# French Bistro

## *Seasonal Recipes*

Bertrand Auboyneau·François Simon

Flammarion

# Contents

*Pages 2–3: The Paul Bert, tables awaiting the diners. Facing page: Details from typically French bistros.*

# The Paul Bert
# with Bertrand Auboyneau

L ife is like a mille-feuille: a many-layered, delectable treat in which sweet is offset by savory, bitter by sour. My life has taken me to many countries: from Africa to the Middle East to Portugal. I was enchanted by the people and geography of each destination: overwhelmed by oppressive heat, struck by dazzling light, and astonished by the vast, empty desert. I was intrigued by the discreet yet omnipresent women, the shared meals, the saffron-yellow mutton, and the teapot passed around the circle. In Portugal, I discovered cilantro, salt cod, and cornbread. In France, I got to know the region of Corrèze, with its reservoirs teeming with fish and its woods where porcini flourish in profusion. Normandy offered up its bucolic farmlands and crème fraîche. My fondness for Brittany began in my childhood and continues today: it came first from my parents and grew through my love for my wife Gwanaëlle and her affection for her family, the sea, and the region.

For over thirty years, wherever I went in the world, I found sanctuary, an urban oasis: the nourishment and comfort that comes with good food, from grilled corn on the cob in Kinshasa and the smile of a Dakar *Mama* to a traditional aromatic *café blanc* in Beirut and pork with clams or cod with olives in the Bairro Alto, in Lisbon. And of course, there is Paris.

I can still taste the slow-cooked leg of lamb that Marc Souverain, renowned architect and expert in vintage cars and beautiful women, prepared one Saturday evening. He owned the Chardenoux restaurant—just sixty feet away from what twenty years later would become the Paul Bert—which was later acquired by the talented, photogenic chef Cyril Lignac. I also remember the sole meunière cooked to perfection by Olivier at Le Villaret. After years of good-humored needling from Michel Picquart, he is now his own boss in the very same kitchen. And what can I say about the succulent headcheese prepared by the grandiose Rodolphe at the Repaire de Cartouche?

Little by little, the emotions awakened by these culinary experiences replaced the preoccupations of my working life. All my feelings were inextricably linked to places with a warm atmosphere, likeable people, unforgettable aromas, endless discussions washed down by good wines. I had fallen in love with food.

The Paul Bert was about to see the light of day. The premises had been occupied by a couscous restaurant, all but abandoned by the tenant, who had lost his shirt (and his soul) in dissolute gambling halls. I slipped a modest tip to the concierge of the building who pointed me in the direction of the owner of the premises. He was from Aveyron, a region of France that was home to many of the traditional Paris bistro owners. He had done well for himself and set up an establishment in the chic suburb of St. Germain-en-Laye. In just an hour, we came to an agreement, and that same evening I became the proud owner of a dis-

*At the Paul Bert, it's not only the food that catches your eye:*
*contrasting styles of tiling also capture your attention.*

gustingly dirty, tastelessly decorated piece of property, with a kitchen that would best be dealt with by demolition. It was also located in a none too desirable area, but none of this worried me in the slightest, for I was in love—twice over. I loved the place, and so did my wife (or at least so she claimed), who declared herself ready for adventure.

After hours of pondering (and many empty bottles later), the most obvious choice for a name came to us: this restaurant, *our* restaurant, would be called the Paul Bert, after the name of the street where it stood. All that was left to do was to create a setting worthy of the bistro I had in mind. We scraped the floors, stripped the walls, sourced antique mercury mirrors, found sets of chairs, varnished tables, and hung vintage posters on the walls. We worked with a winning team: Pierre Sabria, a gruff decorator with a genius for bringing everything together; Michel Tellier, a good-natured craftsman with golden hands; Philippe Bourretz, an antique dealer from Béthune who provided us with period glasses, plates, and dishes that he had inherited from his grandfather, a wholesale dealer in used restaurant supplies; and Jean-Louis Bravo of the well-known flea market in Épinay, who allowed us to pillage his stock of tables, chairs, and other bistro furniture. The first two years were not easy. One cook followed another, none putting in much effort to speak of, none demonstrating the necessary commitment in the kitchen, while we invested our energy and hearts front of house. It didn't look good. Our bank account was redder than our checkered tablecloths, but I held out hope that the good fairies would come up with the goods.

At long last, I found a young chef, fresh from his native region of Morvan in Burgundy. All he knew of Paris at the time was the Périphérique circling the city and the Eiffel Tower. Two interviews later (he replied, "*Oui, monsieur*," to every question), I decided he was the one. It was June, and he needed to give one month's notice to his employer. A week before his start date, he rocked up at the restaurant late at night, more than a little worse for wear, to tell me how happy he was to come and work with me. Things were getting off to a fine start…. Twelve years, countless disagreements, and more than 200,000 clients later, Thierry Laurent is still with us, punctual, smiling, quiet, and conscientious. He's helpful but obstinate; his cooking is precise; he has an eye for the finest products. In short, he is one of the keystones, and not the least important, of our success.

There is one more person who was yet to make an appearance. I owe his contribution to Gwenaëlle's blue eyes. The story goes like this. Our local town hall publishes a magazine, and I'd bought some advertising space. The editor of the magazine suggested that I put myself in the place of a bistro guest and write the text myself. I buckled down and wrote a "review," dwelling on the charms of the blue-eyed waitress. She was not amused…. A few weeks later, a large gentleman with suspenders and sunglasses came in. His first words to me, standing at the bar, were, "Where's the waitress with the blue eyes?" It was Michel Picquart who had just entered the Paul Bert—and my life (but this I would only understand much later). Michel began his career by selling hardware. He then opened two restaurants: Chez Astier and Le Villaret, both in Paris. With Picquart at the reins, both became the gold standard for Parisian "bistronomy". He was known for the fantastic value for money he provided, never skimping on the quality or the provenance of his products. He had an immoderate love for wine, be it white or red, as long as it was good and served correctly. He made it his specialty to serve the most expensive rare wines for next to nothing. He would teach me all this and much more, but I didn't know it then. He entered the Paul Bert, and I fell under his spell.

Yves Camdeborde of Le Comptoir says that Picquart opened his eyes to bistro cuisine, and part of La Régalade's initial success is thanks to him. Pierre Gagnaire, a chef with three Michelin stars, fondly refers to him as "the inspector" and submits to his criticism with a wry smile. The old devil was evangelical in teaching

> *After hours of pondering (and many empty bottles later), the most obvious choice for a name came to us: this resataurant, our restaurant, would be called the Paul Bert, after the name of the street where it stood.*

us about taste—and good taste. He would buzz tirelessly around the streets of Paris on his old scooter hunting down a place for lunch on Mondays (closing day for him), a product to share, or a new chef. Monday lunch was legendary—five to ten friends, all in the restaurant business, would get together. The planning began on the previous Saturday, with countless phone calls, and woe betide the one who dared to cancel on Monday morning. From the most unprepossessing of corner cafés to the most reputed of three-star restaurants, we navigated a veritable maze of eateries, our senses alert, our palates fine-tuned. We went through them all with the same discerning but forgiving fine-toothed comb. As Michel said: "Work is work."

Once the venture was up and running, suitably named and under the protection of our guiding angel, we could enjoy the fruits of our labor by serving good food and fine wine to an appreciative audience, day in and day out. Almost imperceptibly, stealthily, we were transforming an anonymous bistro into the Paul Bert. The wine list, the prices, the napkins, the bar, the plates and silverware, the bread, the waiters' aprons, the type of cream and butter we used, the freshness of the fish, the attention we paid to the season—every decision was made with painstaking care. The guiding principle was the pleasure of our clients—and, of course, our own.

Lastly came my encounter with François Simon, whose formidable presence dominates the industry. We are such good friends today that we can talk about anything at all (even the restaurant business), and that inspired me to work together with him on this book. It is not your typical recipe book, even though it does have recipes, or restaurant guide, even though we do mention some of our favorite addresses. Nor is it a book of photos, even though Christian's photographs are magnificent, or a bible, even if we lay down certain rules. It is not even a book about the Paul Bert, although that is the backdrop. It is a book about the twelve years of happiness we have shared with wonderful people: restaurant owners, wine producers, suppliers, cooks, dishwashers, and waiters, all of whom have contributed to the successful rebirth of the classic bistro.

*Pages 10–11: An aperitif at the Paul Bert with the key players on the Paris bistro scene. Left to right: Gwenaëlle Cadoret of L'Écailler du Bistrot, Gilles Bénard of the Quedubon, Olivier Gaslin of Le Villaret, Francis Bonfilou of the Marsangy, Rodolphe Paquin of the Repaire de Cartouche, Philippe Damas of Philou, Raquel Carena of the Baratin (seated), Bernard Fontenille of L'Abordage, Bertrand Auboyneau, Christophe Acker of the Gorgeon, Benoît Gauthier of Le Grand Pan, and Christophe Dru of Parisian butcher, Boucherie des Provinces. Although not present here, Yves Camdeborde of Le Comptoir, Stéphane Jego of L'Ami Jean, and Cyril Bordarier of Le Verre Volé deserve a special mention as well.*

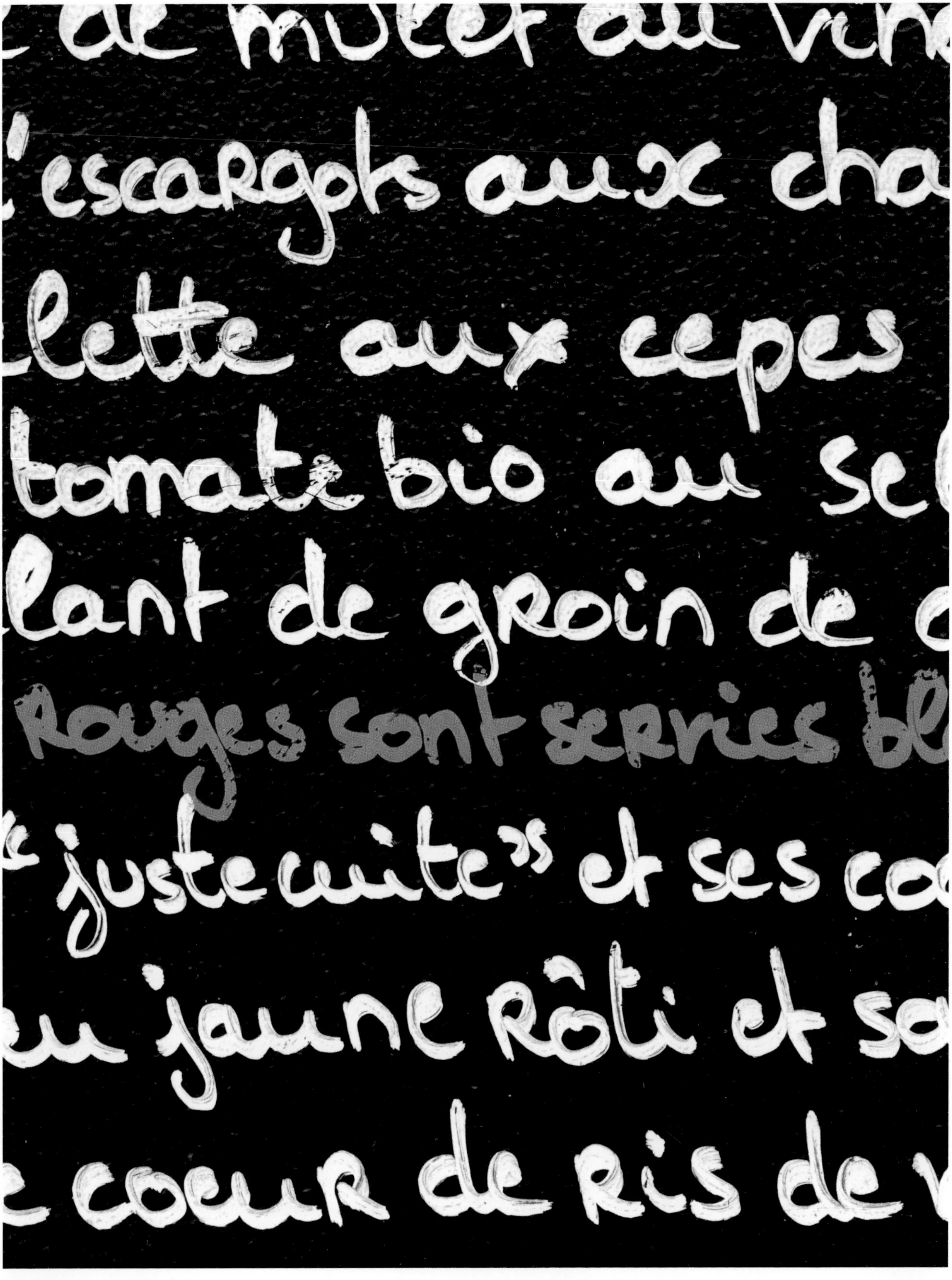

de mulet au vin

'escargots aux cha

lette aux cepes

tomate bio au se

lant de groin de c

Rouges sont serries bl

« juste cuite » et ses co

u jaune Rôti et sa

e coeur de Ris de v

# Introduction
# by François Simon

The bistro is a culinary enclave in the twenty-first century, an institution in parentheses. Think of it, One as an exclamation point. Three coffees, please! Two daily specials! One entrecôte! It speaks to our irrational appetites; it is a social sanctuary: somewhere to reflect, watch passersby, shrug at calories, and mop up the sauce on our plates with good bread. Let the outside world march on in grey suits, they are slaves to their watches. The Paul Bert in Paris illustrates every note of this urban hymn, this calm revolt, this rebellion that runs on salted butter. Bertrand Auboyneau and his wife Gwanaëlle Cadoret have been confidently singing the tune for some twelve years now. A true bistro has a natural melody playing in the background. An ersatz bistro that fakes its chalkboard menus and daily specials can be spotted a mile off. And the clients are no fools. It's like a second-rate pop tune, catchy but soulless. They may go to one of these "phony" bistros once but will never go back. The Paul Bert, just like a string of other genuine bistros, continues to be a success because of its genuine respect for both its food and diners. You will feel it as you enter and taste it in the crunch of the bread and the thickness of the entrecôte. But there is nothing laid-back about the welcoming ambience and the exemplary menu. A bistro is hard labor, sweat, and toil. It requires getting up at the crack of dawn, smiling through minor disasters, and, even if the catch of the day is poor, motivating the team, welcoming the guests, slicing the bread, and waiting until lingering clients have downed the last drops in their champagne flutes.

The bistro is one of the last remaining venues of live theater in our cities. Clients take their positions without prompting, talk to strangers at the bar, ask their neighbors to pass the salt, scrounge a smoke outside, and maybe even leave with a cell phone number. The bistro is the setting against which minor dramas and romances are played out. The director asks only that the actors enjoy life, laugh, tell stories, and savor their delicious fare. The bistro sings a serious yet light-hearted chorus. The generosity of Bertrand and Gwenaëlle has inspired us to write this book in which they confide their secrets, recipes, and tales.

*The daily chalkboard menu reveals both the chef's mood and the season at the Paul Bert.*

# The Ten Bistro Essentials

# The Owner

*The essential ingredient for a good bistro*

Bertrand Auboyneau belongs to a generation of bistro owners that straddles two centuries; these owners draw their strength from the perspective this gives them. They have had the good sense not to wipe the slate clean, keeping the best of the past, and have made a wise selection from all that is presently on offer. The clientele comes seeking the archetypal bistro. Bertrand Auboyneau has succeeded admirably in meeting these expectations, concocting his own inimitable recipe for an immensely satisfying serving of the bistro experience.

The bistro owner does not just preside from behind the bar. For one thing, there is hardly room to set a stool there, let alone a throne. Watch him in action, and see him slipping smoothly from behind the bar into the dining area, gliding between tables to his kitchen destination. He is a ringmaster, a middleman between artist and spectators. He is master at manipulating the rapport, hyping up the image of the former (the chef) and titillating the latter (the client). The ringmaster is no mere server. He is a sounding board, a magician (albeit without the top hat) with endless tricks up his sleeve. He must sense instinctively which table requires his presence, which would like him to stop by for a chat, and which prefers privacy. He will linger, bring personally a plate or two, or advise on a particular vintage of wine. The owner is the focal point of the bistro. Clients come for him, for his cheeky humor, for his presence. They take refuge under his tutelage. He sums up the soul of the bistro in his person, defining it with his sunny or foul temperament. For owners embody the entire range of human nature, and the character of the owner colors the character of his establishment, setting its spirit and its noise level. There are calm owners who exude a bourgeois charm; others are noisier and more stereotypically Gallic. Some speak in hushed tones, wear tweeds, and communicate discreetly with a nod. A bistro owner's personality will give you a fair idea of the register of

*Thierry Laurent, the exemplary Paul Bert chef, allows the fame of the bistro to take center stage while he works in the background. His ingenuity provides the Paul Bert with its remarkable seasonal menus.*

his cuisine. There are owners who are shrewd, reserved, or complicated. The contents of the plate usually follow their style.

Some come for the rough treatment that the owner bestows on clients, while others prefer their privacy. There are tables for lovers and tables for unsociable types who just want to stay in their corner. It's up to the owner to sniff them out, to sense exactly what distance the clients require. There's no point in asking them if everything is all right because that goes without saying. The question that might annoy them would brighten up the day of the guests at the neighboring table.

The bistro owner is the one who knows. This is not an extract from the book of maxims of the bar (Article 1: The chef is always right; Article 2: The chef is always right.) Quite the contrary: the chef is always wrong. Or rather, the owner is the one who knows what the right dish is, what his clientele wants (it changes from one neighborhood to another), and exactly what his chef is good at. And with all this in mind, he has to set his course and keep to it. Does he want traditional bourgeois cooking or "bistronomy"? Would he prefer it a bit rough around the edge or more delicate and feminine, light or copious? It's up to the owner to decide on his brand and keep to it. The chef should follow in his trail, contributing his talent without going too far, otherwise there's the danger that the bistro might turn out badly and become … of all things, a restaurant!

# Organic Tomato, Anchovy, Black Olive, and Arugula Salad, Niçoise-Style

**SERVES 4**

- 24 raw anchovy fillets
- 2 beefheart tomatoes
- 2 Black Krim tomatoes (Ukrainian heirloom tomatoes)
- 2 green tomatoes
- 2 yellow tomatoes
- 2 mild red onions
- 2 shallots
- 2 slices sandwich loaf
- Olive oil as needed
- 2 oz. (50 g) arugula
- 24 black olives, pitted
- 1 tablespoon plus 1 teaspoon (20 ml) sherry vinegar
- 4 hardboiled eggs
- 12 long-stemmed caper berries

**PREPARATION**

A day ahead, season the anchovy fillets on both sides with salt and pepper, and chill.

The next day, cut the tomatoes into pieces, and finely slice the onions and shallots into rings.

To make the croutons, dice the slices of bread into small cubes, and sauté them with a little olive oil in a pan until they are nice and crusty.

Arrange the tomatoes, arugula, and black olives in individual bowls. Add the vinegar and olive oil. Then quarter the hardboiled eggs, and place them atop the salad with the croutons. Top with the anchovy fillets, and garnish with the onion and shallot rings and the caper berries.

# Home-Style White Asparagus

**SERVES 4**

- 20–24 white asparagus stalks
- 15 sprigs tarragon
- 15 sprigs flat-leaf parsley
- 3 or 4 hardboiled eggs
- Olive oil as needed
- 2 oz (60 g) Parmesan shavings

**PREPARATION**

Peel the asparagus, and cook them in lightly salted boiling water.

Chop the tarragon and parsley.

Roughly crumble the hardboiled eggs using a fork, so that the egg whites and yolks mix.

Carefully combine the chopped herbs with the crumbled eggs, drizzling in a little olive oil.

Arrange the asparagus on a plate, spoon the egg mixture over them, and sprinkle with the Parmesan shavings.

**A dash of advice**

The best way to cook asparagus is to tie them into bunches and place them upright in a pot of boiling water with their tips peeking out above the surface.

# The Bar: A Solid Foundation

What would a bistro be without its bar? It is the rock upon which the bistro is built—maybe that is why people cling to it like a port in a storm. They hold on to it for dear life, as if it (or they) might otherwise fly away. It's a solid construction: the combined weight of its lead, zinc, and heavy wood anchor it solidly to the floor. It seems to have been there long enough to grow roots, drawing strength and serenity from its grounded solidity. The bar must be at elbow level, never low enough for children—no children allowed at the bar. The bar is subjected to thumps, knocks, and wipes. It is impervious to parting words, endless chatter, bygones being bygones, and slates being wiped clean. It listens with a kindly ear to human suffering and passing fortunes. The bar is often located near the entrance, standing like a watchtower or a concierge's lodge. The concierge, in this case, is the owner, and he considers this strategic location to be the symbol of his power and reign. The bar is a benevolent entity, a latter-day confessional. Feel free to open your heart there (unless you're a smoker, in which case go outside). When the time comes, you can leave the safety of the bar for the comfort of your table.

*The bar is both focal point and watchtower.*
*You're tempted to stay, but your awaiting table beckons....*

# Veal Chop in a Creamed Morel Sauce with Homemade Mashed Potatoes

**SERVES 4**

- Four 14-oz. (400-g) bone-in veal chops
- 3 ½ oz. (100 g) dried morels
- ⅔ cup (150 ml) milk
- 7 tablespoons (100 g) butter, divided
- 2 shallots, chopped
- ¾ cup (200 ml) heavy or double cream
- Salt and freshly ground pepper
- Freshly grated nutmeg

**PREPARATION**

A day ahead, re-hydrate the morels by leaving them to soak in a scant ¼ cup milk in the refrigerator overnight.

To prepare the meat, brown the veal chops in a skillet with half the butter for 5 to 6 minutes on each side. Set them aside in a warm place.

Fry the shallots until lightly browned in the remaining butter. Stir in the cream, and cook for 5 more minutes. Then add the morels, and simmer over low heat for another 5 minutes. Return the veal chops to the skillet, and cook for 2 to 5 minutes, depending on desired doneness. Remove the chops when they are cooked to your satisfaction, and arrange them on the plates. Reduce the sauce if necessary, and adjust the seasoning. Don't forget to add a little grated nutmeg just before serving.

See page 106 for the mashed potatoes.

**A dash of advice**

If the provenance of the veal chops isn't impeccable, they don't make the cut. An unsavory practice persists of exporting calves born on French soil to other parts of Europe, where they are slaughtered in hellish conditions, then exported back to France, vacuum-packed with the ambiguous designation "*Issus de la CEE*" (Product of the EEC), for sale on the French market. The Paul Bert encourages French consumers to support French farmers who breed and rear their calves to full size and who, bound by stringent regulations, maintain excellent production standards. This is the type of veal for which this recipe was intended, and which, when cooked until perfectly pink and topped with a few truffle shavings or chanterelles, creates a truly memorable dish.

# Milk-Fed Lamb and Baby Vegetable Pot Roast

**SERVES 4**

- Two 2 ½-lb. (1.2-kg) shoulders of lamb
- 2 carrots
- 4 small round turnips
- 2 potatoes
- 8 small leeks
- 8 pearl onions
- 2 zucchini (courgettes)

- 12 white button mushrooms
- 3 ½ tablespoons (50 g) unsalted butter
- 1 onion
- Scant ½ cup (100 ml) dry white wine
- 1 bouquet garni (thyme, bay leaf, and 20 sprigs fresh sage)
- Scant ½ cup (100 ml) water

**PREPARATION**

Cut the vegetables into 1-in. (3-cm) pieces, and set aside.

Brown the lamb shoulders in butter on all sides in a large cast-iron pot.

Chop the onion, and add it to the pot.

Deglaze with white wine, add the bouquet garni, and pour in the water. Simmer for 10 to 25 minutes, depending on desired doneness.

Transfer the meat to a dish, and keep in a warm place. Filter the cooking liquid, and return it to the pot. Cook the vegetables in the following order, adding each one 10 minutes after the previous one: the carrots together with the turnips, then the potatoes, then the leeks with the pearl onions, and lastly the zucchini with the mushrooms. Mix them together. Keep a careful eye on them as they cook; check to see if they are cooked by pricking them lightly. When the vegetables are done, return the meat to the pot, and bring it all to the table.

A dash of advice

- Choose whoever is fooling around at the table to slice the meat.
- Our wine chalkboard features *vins nature*—untreated wines—specially chosen to go with the dishes of the day in case you can't be bothered to study the wine list.

*A wine list in memory of Sébastien Alessandri, who opened the Paul Bert with me. An outstanding Corsican cook and a pioneer in the search for natural wines well before they became fashionable, Alessandri sadly left us too soon.*

## The Paul Bert

The bistro is not yet open, but the team has already been busy for hours, unpacking the market delivery and other orders in the kitchen and preparing the dining area. Laetitia carefully writes up the day's menu. The chalkboard is a good indicator of the quality of a bistro. If it is too static, the regular guests will tire of it, but if it changes too often, they might feel frustrated. And if a favorite dish disappears altogether.... It's a fine line between tradition and innovation.

# Chocolate Soufflé

**SERVES 4**

For this recipe, it's particularly important to weigh the ingredients accurately.

- 4 cups (1 l) milk
- 7 oz. (200 g) egg yolks
- ¾ cup (5 ¼ oz./150 g) granulated sugar
- 3 tablespoons plus ¼ teaspoon (1 oz./30 g) custard powder
- ½ oz. (16 g) bittersweet chocolate, 70 percent cocoa

- 2 ¼ tablespoons (½ oz./16 g) unsweetened cocoa powder
- 4 ½ oz. (125 g) egg whites
- Pinch salt
- ¾ cup (5 ¼ oz./150 g) granulated sugar for the egg whites
- A little butter to grease the molds or ramekins

**PREPARATION**

Bring the milk to a boil. Beat the egg yolks with the sugar and custard powder until the mixture is thick and pale. Gradually pour the hot milk over this mixture, whisking as you do so, and return it all to the heat. Cook over low heat until it thickens, about 6 to 10 minutes. Add the chocolate and cocoa powder (you might want to sift it in), and mix thoroughly. Leave to cool slightly—it should be warm for the next stage.

Preheat the oven to 350°F (180°C). Whisk the egg whites with the salt and sugar using an electric beater until they form stiff peaks. Fold the warm cream mixture into the beaten egg whites.

Grease the molds or ramekins well with butter, pour in the mixture to just under ½ in. (1 cm) below each ramekin rim, and bake for 12 minutes. The soufflés should rise to about 1 to 1 ½ in. (2–4 cm) above the rims of the ramekins. Serve immediately.

# Old-Fashioned Rice Pudding with Dulce de Leche

**SERVES 4**

- 5 oz. (150 g) Arborio rice
- 1 Tahiti vanilla bean
- 1 cup (250 ml) whole milk
- 2 tablespoons (25 g) granulated sugar

- 2 teaspoons (10 g) butter
- 1 egg yolk
- 3 generous tablespoons *dulce de leche*

**PREPARATION**

Six hours ahead, slit the vanilla bean lengthwise, and scrape the seeds into the milk. Leave the whole bean to infuse with the milk for at least 6 hours in the refrigerator.

Parboil the rice in boiling water for 5 minutes. Drain it, and set it to cook over low heat with the vanilla-scented milk. Add the sugar, and leave for about 25 minutes, stirring regularly.

When the rice is cooked (it should be very soft but not completely mushy), stir in the butter, egg yolk, and 2 generous tablespoons of *dulce de leche*. Just before serving, garnish with another spoon of *dulce de leche*.

A dash of advice

- *Dulce de leche* is a sort of milk jam from Argentina. If it is unavailable locally, cook Nestlé sweetened condensed milk slowly over low heat until it is slightly caramelized.
- Arborio rice is also used to make risotto—it absorbs liquid well when cooked.

# The Chef

*Caught in the cross fire*

*The serving hatch at the Paul Bert provides a picturesque frame for the evening's dishes. The orders from each table flutter in the steam of the plates.*

If you want to know who's behind a successful establishment, just sniff out the nearest victim. In the bistro, it's easy. Who slaves over a hot stove thirty-six hours a day, juggles the work of eight, and endures the rages of the owner and the impatience of the clients? You guessed it—it's the chef. A latter-day St. Sebastian, the chef suffers in silence. He has to be some sort of saint in order to put up with that curious species known as *the client*, who arrives too late, shows up too early, demands different side dishes, wants his meat either overdone or underdone, who lingers, is in too much of a hurry (the chef's job would be so much easier if there were no clients....). And then there is the owner, a domestic tyrant who, even if he doesn't quite think he's God, certainly seems to act like he is at times. The chef of a bistro is like a swimmer whose swimsuit has been weighed down with lead. He has phenomenal abs and the suppleness of a gymnast. He has to juggle his stock of knowledge, his wishes, his ambition, the owner, and the clients. So he swims underwater, bound to the stove, tucked away in the steam and the neon light. The bistro chef is a superman, made of one part humility, one part patience, and one part admirable self-sacrifice. Should he be seized with a sudden desire to surprise the clients with his own signature dish, the owner is there to steer him back on course, lighten a recipe, or temper the spiciness of a sauce. There is a constant struggle between the two men: a potential talent

*A bistro's secret weapon
is tucked away in the kitchen:
Thierry Laurent at the
Paul Bert, Raquel Carena
at the Baratin, Stéphane Jego
at L'Ami Jean, and Francis
Bonfilou at the Marsangy.*

just wating to shine and a calm and stoic lion tamer, swaggering in his swanky clothes but also caught in the middle of his public and the artist. This must be why bistro cuisine is a genre that is so darn well put together: it is no-nonsense and to the point. It avoids the narcissism of restaurants, their emblazoned haughtiness and monogrammed decadence, opting for a down-to-earth, homespun cuisine—the kind an increasingly well-informed clientele is willing to seek out. Bistros are a roaring success in Paris today due to their moderation, the culinary wisdom that the unlikely pair of owner and chef delivers. For all this, the chef is not second-best or a downtrodden Cinderella. He may not be in the spotlight, but he has the tranquil force of a navigator. He knows all too well that without him, the car would go off the road. Is he indispensable? Not really: no one is indispensable in a bistro. Bistro cuisine is so successful because under the hood is a finely tuned engine ready to accelerate. An average restaurant serves from sixty to one hundred clients a day, while a bistro like the Paul Bert serves from 180 to 200 clients. Like a top-of-the-range motor, its formidable power is barely audible when it's idling. A pâté en croûte at opening time is like the low growling of a sports car at a stop sign. It's the clients' good fortune to have a pilot behind the wheel of such high-performance machines. Without him, they would have their pâté en croûte with asparagus Chantilly and a square-shaped dollop of garden pea foam. Bistro clients don't know how lucky they are.

# Salt-Cod-Filled Piquillo Peppers

**SERVES 4**

- 7 oz. (200 g) salt cod
- 14 oz. (400 g) potatoes, suitable for mashing
- Scant ¼ cup (50 ml) crème fraîche
- ¾ cup (200 ml) Sicilian olive oil
- 1 bunch cilantro (coriander) leaves
- 16 *piquillo* peppers
- Salt and freshly ground pepper

**PREPARATION**

A day ahead, soak the salt cod in cold water for 24 hours, changing the water at least three times, to remove some of the salt.

The next day, boil the potatoes in lightly salted water, and press them through a mill. Then incorporate the crème fraîche.

Place the salt cod in a saucepan with enough cold water to cover it, and bring to the boil with the lid on. Continue to cook for 6 to 8 minutes, then drain it, and shred it finely.

Preheat the oven to 350°F (180°C).

Carefully combine the cod with the mashed potatoes, taking care not to crush the fish.

Snip the cilantro, and add it to the mixture. Adjust the seasoning. Fill the *piquillo* peppers with the mixture. Drizzle them with a little olive oil, and cook for 5 minutes in the oven.

A dash of advice

You'll find *piquillo* peppers in gourmet stores. The authentic peppers are from northern Spain.

# Pollock Tartare with Green Apples, Japanese Vinegar, and Aged Soy Sauce

**SERVES 4**

- 1 lb. (500 g) extremely fresh pollock fillet
- Scant ½ cup (100 ml) olive oil
- Citrus-scented Japanese vinegar
- Aged fermented soy sauce
- 1 nicely tart Granny Smith apple
- Salt and freshly ground pepper

**PREPARATION**

First, check that there are no bones in the fish fillets. Carefully cut the pollock into cubes—they should not be too small, about ½ in. (1 cm), so that the tartare retains enough texture.

Place the diced fish in a mixing bowl, and add the oil and vinegar. Season with salt and pepper, and mix gently. Chill for 15 minutes.

Finely slice the apple—leave it unpeeled. Spoon the fish tartare onto the plates, and top with the apple slices. Dab drops of aged soy sauce around the tartare.

A dash of advice

The quality of the vinegar and soy sauce are all-important here. If you're in Paris, stop by the Issé boutique, which specializes in fine Japanese groceries.

# Duck Foie Gras Marbled with Leeks

**SERVES 8 TO 10**

- 2 lb. (1 kg) raw duck foie gras
- 9 lb. (4 kg) medium-sized leeks
- 2 cups (½ l) clear chicken stock
- 6 sheets (12 g) gelatin sheets (available online or at specialty stores)

- 1 teaspoon (5 g) salt
- 1 ½ teaspoons (5 g) freshly ground pepper
- Scant ½ cup (100 ml) olive oil
- 2 tablespoons (30 ml) balsamic vinegar

**PREPARATION**

Heat the chicken stock. Soften the gelatin sheets in lukewarm water. When they have softened, wring out the excess water, and incorporate them into the hot stock. Leave to cool until it is barely warm (this is the temperature required to assemble the terrine).

Cook the leeks in boiling salted water. Cool them down immediately in ice water, so that they retain their green color. Drain them, and press them gently over a colander to remove as much water as possible.

Cut the whites of the leeks to the length of the terrine (about 8 in./20 cm).

Remove the veins from the foie gras, and cut it into very thin slices, about ⅛ in. (5 mm) thick. Heat a pan, and rapidly cook the sliced foie gras, 10 seconds on each side. Set aside on a paper towel to drain. Season with salt and pepper. Line the terrine with plastic wrap. If you wish, you can line the terrine with the greens of the leeks. Then alternate a layer of leeks with a layer of foie gras, each time pouring in a ladle of barely warm stock, finishing with a layer of leeks.

Wrap tightly with plastic wrap, and chill for 24 hours.

*A dash of advice*

- To make the chicken stock, you can use a stock cube.
- You can replace the balsamic vinegar with sour cider vinegar.
- This staple recipe at the Paul Bert was created by my son Thomas, who now has a restaurant in Tokyo. It pairs wonderfully with a bottle of white wine made by Agnès and René Mosse, artisan winemakers in Saint-Lambert-du-Lattey in the Loire region.

## Michel Picquart: Forefather of the Modern Bistro

Back in the day, he used to introduce himself as a hardware salesman. Michel Picquart did in fact once own a store selling nuts and bolts near the place de la République in Paris. On the side, he would cook for his customers and employees. And then one day, bored with a life he found as predictable as a tape measure, he sold his store to his employees and, cash in hand, made his way to the restaurant Chez Astier, where the woman who owned it taught him the basics of Béarnaise sauce and sole meunière. He discovered the joys of the bistro, launching the first bistro set menu (starter-main course-dessert) in Paris. This was back in the 1980s; the bistro trend was set to blossom with Yves Camdeborde's Le Comptoir, opened in 1992, and other new-generation chefs straight out of luxury hotels. "Picquart taught me everything," says Bertrand Auboyneau. "Without him, there would have been no Paul Bert." He taught him that idiosyncratic bistro-speak, or bartender slang, as well as his perspective on generosity. It was this that led Michel Picquart to sell Chez Astier to his employees. He did the same with Le Villaret, handing it over to his team when he was sixty-three years old, before he was summoned to the great kitchen in the sky.

*At Le Villaret, near the place de la République in Paris, a picture of the late Michel Picquart, the epitome of the bistro spirit, gazes out at diners.*

## Le Villaret

*The façade of Le Villaret is very discreet, almost anonymous. For a long time, its name wasn't even visible. This understated style should be reassuring: it is a sign of the establishment's confidence, and, indeed, the restaurant is never empty. The key to its success? A seasonal menu concocted by Olivier Gaslin and complemented by a remarkable wine list.*

# Roasted Suckling Pig with Dried Apricots and Touquet New Potatoes

**SERVES 4 TO 6**

- 2 hams of suckling pig, plus the rack (have your butcher cut the hams into 8 pieces each)
- ½ lb. (250 g) trimmings of suckling pig, not too fatty, and 2 lb. (1 kg) bones
- 7 tablespoons (100 g) butter, divided
- 1 onion, unpeeled, studded with 2 cloves
- 1 leek, greens remaining
- 1 stalk celery
- 4 cloves garlic, chopped

- 2 onions, chopped
- 1 cup (250 ml) white wine
- 2 sprigs thyme, 2 bay leaves, and 2 sprigs rosemary
- 5 oz. (150 g) dried apricots
- 14 oz. (400 g) new potatoes, preferably *rattes* (Touquet variety) or other fingerling potatoes
- 3 shallots, chopped
- 15 sprigs flat-leaf parsley
- Salt and freshly ground pepper

**PREPARATION**

First make the pork stock: cook the bones and trimmings with a third of the butter in a 350°F (180°C) oven until they are nicely browned. Transfer them, scraping up all the juices, to a pot with a bouquet garni (the unpeeled onion studded with cloves, the leek, and the celery stalk, securely tied together with a length or two of kitchen twine). Pour in 6 cups (1.5 l) water, and leave to simmer for 2 hours. Skim the top regularly as the boiling progresses. Then leave to reduce by half. You should have about 2 cups (500 ml) of pork stock.

Melt another third of the butter in an ovenproof pot over high heat, and brown the pieces of ham and the rack. Add two cloves of garlic and the chopped onions. Deglaze with the white wine; add the thyme, bay leaves, and a sprig of rosemary; and pour in the pork stock, so that it half-covers the contents.

Place the pot in a 350°F (180°C) oven, cover with the lid, and cook for 20 minutes, spooning the juices over the meat regularly. When the meat is cooked, remove the pieces, keeping them in a warm place, and strain the sauce through a fine-mesh sieve. Reduce it by about half in a clean saucepan, add the apricots to heat them through, and adjust the seasoning.

Sauté the potatoes in the remaining butter with the remaining two cloves of garlic, shallots, and a sprig of rosemary. Arrange the pork, apricots, and potatoes in a dish, and scatter with freshly chopped flat-leaf parsley.

A dash of advice

A true suckling pig should weigh between 13 ½ and 15 ¼ lb. (6 to 7 kg). Personally, I prefer them a little plumper: when they weigh in at about 22 lb. (10 kg). The flesh is then more mature and even tastier. Thyme, rosemary, and dried apricots served with a crisp suckling pig call for a wine from the South of France, one that is full-bodied with a long finish. Le Bois des Merveilles, from Jean-Baptiste Senat's magnificent estate in the Minervois region, is just what the doctor ordered.

# Strawberry Macaroons

**MAKES 8 TO 10 MACAROONS**

For this recipe, it's particularly important to weigh the ingredients accurately.

*For the macaroons:*

- 2 cups (6 oz./175 g) ground almonds
- 2 ½ cups (11 ½ oz./325 g) confectioners' sugar
- 5 ½ oz. (160 g) egg whites (about 5 ½ egg whites, but do weigh them)
- 1 tablespoon plus 2 teaspoons (⅔ oz./20 g) granulated sugar
- Pinch salt
- Juice of ½ lemon
- 2 teaspoons (10 ml) red food coloring

*For the Chantilly cream:*

- ½ cup (125 ml) whipping cream, 30–35 percent butterfat
- 2 ½ tablespoons (1 oz./30 g) granulated sugar
- 2 teaspoons (10 ml) red food coloring

*For the filling:*

- ½ lb. (250 g) strawberries

**PREPARATION**

First prepare the macaroons. Sift the ground almonds with the confectioners' sugar.

Whisk the egg whites with the granulated sugar, salt, lemon juice, and food coloring until they form firm peaks.

Carefully fold the sifted almond mixture into the egg whites using a flexible spatula. Then spoon the batter into a pastry bag.

Preheat the oven to 285°F (140°C). Line a baking sheet with parchment paper, and pipe out 2-in. (5-cm) diameter macaroons. Leave them to rest for 30 minutes at room temperature, then bake for 20 minutes.

Next prepare the Chantilly cream. With an electric beater, whip the cream with the sugar and food coloring until it forms a Chantilly consistency. Spoon it into a pastry bag.

To finish, take one macaroon, and arrange a circle of strawberries around it. Pipe out some Chantilly cream into the center. Top with another macaroon, pressing lightly to spread the cream out evenly. Repeat with the remaining macaroon shells.

A dash of advice

Strawberries, raspberries, red currants, and mulberries are all redolent of summer vacations and afternoons picking fruit in our gardens. The seasonality of ingredients is crucial: forget those that arrive in mid-winter from the other side of the globe. We need to learn to wait for them. Seasonal ingredients are the lifeblood of our bistros. After the berries, the melons and cherries will arrive. Even here, life follows the cycle of the seasons.

Baba au Rhum façon sava
Macaron aux Fraises
Ile Flottante aux praline
soufflé au grand marni
glaces et sorbets maison

ENTRÉE: 8€ + supl PLAT: 21,

la maison n'acc                    èques

## The Baratin

*From its hilltop in the Belleville district, the Baratin has a wonderful view of the city. Behind the bistro's deceptively simple façade awaits the surprisingly creative, no-nonsense cuisine of Raquel Carena, who cooks from the heart. Her instinctive cooking is unique. The service and wine, courtesy of Philippe Pinoteau, are an additional source of delight for the clientele of this restaurant, where celebrities from the worlds of literature, cinema, and fashion mingle.*

# The Chalkboard Menu

*Market products*

*The strength of bistro cooking owes much to its flexibility. The chalkboard menu attests to its adaptability. Far more than a rustic decorative feature, the chalkboard reflects the economic preoccupations of a cuisine based on market availability and fluctuating commodity prices. Should a certain fish suddenly become plentiful, the chef and the owner will immediately modify the day's menu. Unlike grand restaurants bound by a printed menu and an established reputation, the renown of a bistro flies on the winds of change.*

Unlike restaurants and brasseries, where the menu is printed for the year, the bistro is in a state of constant flux. It changes according to what's available at the market—and to the whim of the owner who keeps his eyes peeled for fresh ideas. If the price of a certain fish skyrockets, the owner will be off to find something else, unlike in a restaurant, where the chef would simply have to continue reproducing his signature dishes, whatever the price of the fish. The bistro is lucky enough to be able to seize opportunities as they arise, though it must remain faithful to its fundamental principles at the same time. It's hard to imagine certain bistros without their eggs with mayonnaise, pâté en croûte, or herring and potato salad. The bistro works by habit. You go because you're sure to find your usual steak with mustard, sole meunière, or favorite dried sausage. If it's not there, the charm instantly evaporates. Bistro dishes are shareable: blanquette, pot-au-feu, *lapin à la moutarde*. These one-pot dishes call for conviviality. After all, when you eat the same dish, you can really say that you are eating *together*. The affability is tangible in the down-to-earth dishes, the ones that everyone likes.

It is a cuisine free of complexes, making a meal of offal or turning out value-for-money dishes from forgotten or under-valued cuts of meat—or even leftovers, like the Parmentier. The bistro is opportunistic, making the most of seasonal produce and market stands. Should a tray of ripe yellow plums

pschitt.

Entrée + Plat
ou Plat + Dessert      26 €

Entrée + Plat + Dessert      32 € prix nets,

- Millefeuilles d'avocat aux écrevisses
- Salade de bulots à l'aïoli
- Terrine de lapin maison
- Salade de boeuf à l'estragon
- Foie gras de canard maison (+3€)
- Jambon persillé de Bourgogne
- Terrine de soie en gelée
- Salade de langoustines fraîches (+3€)

- Bavette de boeuf poêlée nature ou sauce au poivre
- Pintade fermière rôtie à l'estragon
- Rognon de veau à la crème de morilles (+3€)
- Paleron de boeuf en cocotte

*From the chalkboard menu at the Marsangy (page 55), to the amazing restaurant-cum-boutique of La Tête dans les Olives (above, left and right) and the Boucherie des Provinces next to the bustling Aligre market (above, center), the inspiration of a bistro menu responds to the whims of nature. Morel mushrooms, seasonal vegetables, a crisp head of lettuce, fine olive oil… and a new dish is born.*

suddenly appear, they will be transformed into the tart of the day. There is a spontaneity born of functionality in bistro cuisine; it is optimistic by nature. This is why the chalkboard menu is the barometer of what's happening in the kitchen. It travels from table to table; it is taken by the sides and balanced on a chair. If a dish's ingredients are exhausted, it's erased immediately. But don't believe that the chalkboard automatically means everything is fresh. It's also a device used by some cunning restaurateurs who shamelessly have ready-made dishes delivered to the kitchen door by big business—steer clear if you can spot them.

Bistro cooking is no longer exclusively found in bistros these days. For some years now, upscale restaurants have taken to "revisiting" bistro recipes, gussying up old standbys. That's fine: bistro cooking can take the competition. It doesn't mind being used as inspiration for the great and the good. Perhaps it will even help the grand restaurants win back members of the public who have been avoiding them.

Bistro cuisine has its own "punctuation," invigorating little tidbits, such as gherkins, mustard, and Béarnaise sauce. Bistro cooking kicks up its heels and gallops along. The bistro contents itself with providing the cuisine of the moment and is happy to let others wear themselves out pursuing immortality.

# Country Pâté with Pickled Chanterelles

**SERVES 8**

*For the terrine:*
- 4 lb. (2 kg) fatty pork cut, such as blade shoulder (US) or spare ribs (UK)
- 1 lb. (500 g) pork liver
- 1 lb. (500 g) chicken liver
- 2 cloves garlic
- 6 shallots
- 1 bunch flat-leaf parsley
- 5 sprigs thyme, leaves picked off
- 3 tablespoons plus 1 teaspoon (50 ml) cognac

- 1 cup (250 ml) whipping cream, 30–35 percent butterfat
- 2 eggs, beaten
- 7 teaspoons (1 ¼ oz./36 g) salt
- 1 tablespoon (9 g) freshly ground pepper
- 1 bay leaf

*For the slow-cooked chanterelles:*
- 5 oz. (150 g) very small chanterelles
- 1 tablespoon plus 1 teaspoon (20 g) butter

- 2 shallots
- 1 clove garlic
- 2 bay leaves
- ¾ cup (200 ml) sherry vinegar
- Salt and freshly ground pepper

*Special equipment needed:*
- A cooking or meat thermometer
- A glass jar (this will be sterilized when the boiling vinegar is poured in)

**PREPARATION**

Prepare both the terrine and the slow-cooked chanterelles two to three days ahead.

First prepare the terrine. Grind the pork meat, pork liver, and chicken livers in a mincing machine using the coarse screen. Chop the garlic, shallots, and parsley.

Place the ground meats in a large mixing bowl, and add the thyme, cognac, cream, chopped shallots, garlic, parsley, and beaten eggs. Season with the salt and pepper.

Mix all the ingredients together well, and place the mixture in a terrine, topping it with the bay leaf.

Preheat the oven to 350°F (180°C). Place the terrine in a large dish half-filled with water to create a bain-marie, and cook in the heated oven for approximately 45 minutes, or until the core temperature reaches 175°F (80°C). Use a thermometer to verify.

When it is ready, remove the terrine from the oven, and place a weight firmly over it (after protecting it with aluminum foil, for example) for 15 minutes.

When the terrine has cooled, refrigerate it for two to three days.

To prepare the slow-cooked chanterelles, wash the chanterelles briefly under running water, and dry them using a clean cloth.

Sauté them lightly in the butter, and season with salt and pepper.

Finely chop the shallots and garlic, and place them into the glass jar, along with the 2 bay leaves.

Bring the sherry vinegar to a boil in a saucepan. Add the sautéed chanterelles to the jar, and pour the boiling vinegar over them.

Tightly shut the jar, and allow the contents to cool, before placing in the refrigerator for two to three days. Then serve.

*A dash of advice*

- We serve this terrine with slices of toasted country bread.
- Use the highest-quality vinegar available.
- If you wish, add a sprig of thyme to the pickling jar.

# Sarawak Pepper Tuna, Mi-Cuit

**SERVES 4 TO 5**

- 1 lb. 5 oz. (600 g) tuna fillet (ask your fish seller for a long piece with, if possible, no dark parts)
- About 2 heaped tablespoons (⅔ oz./20 g) Sarawak pepper
- 2 teaspoons (10 g) salt
- ⅔ cup (150 ml) olive oil, divided
- 5 oz. (150 g) red currants
- 1 teaspoon aged soy sauce
- A few arugula and baby spinach leaves

**PREPARATION**

Crush the pepper by hand with a mortar and pestle—the advantage of this method is that it does not heat the pepper, so all the flavor is retained.

Roll the tuna fillet in the crushed pepper and salt until it is entirely coated. Heat a pan, and sear the fillet quickly all over in one-third of the olive oil. Then leave it to cool.

Roll it tightly in plastic wrap to form a 2 ½–3-in. (5–7-cm) diameter sausage shape. Place it in the refrigerator.

Using a fork, crush the red currants in a bowl. Stir in the aged soy sauce and the remaining olive oil, and combine well.

Cut the tuna into rounds, and serve with the arugula and spinach leaves, all seasoned with the red currant vinaigrette.

A dash of advice

When making this recipe, it's important to bear in mind that Mediterranean bluefin tuna, captured in vast conical nets and fattened in offshore sea cages, should no longer be invited to our tables. Not only is it overfished, the fishing linked to bluefin tuna farming destroys the stocks of numerous other oily fish, such as mackerel, sardines, and anchovies. However, there are many other excellent types of red-fleshed tuna available.

## The Paul Bert

*In a few minutes, the bistro will open. The tables are standing at attention, and the chairs are lined up. But you've just missed one of the crucial moments in the life of a bistro: the arrival of the day's produce. Not long ago, crates of fruit and vegetables and hunks of meat were being ferried into the kitchen. Now, it's the quiet before the storm: the guests are about to arrive!*

# Porcini Fricassee

**SERVES 4**

- 10 oz. (300 g) young porcini
- 3 ½ tablespoons (50 g) butter
- 1 clove garlic, chopped
- 15 sprigs parsley, chopped
- Salt and freshly ground pepper

**PREPARATION**

Peel the porcini under running water. Dry them thoroughly, and cut them in half.

Melt the butter in a pan over high heat. When it is foaming, add the porcini, and fry for about 10 minutes. Add the chopped garlic and parsley. Season with salt and pepper, and serve.

# Herring and Potato Salad

**SERVES 4**

- 8 wood-smoked herring fillets
- 10 oz. (300 g) new potatoes, preferably *rattes* (Touquet variety) or other fingerling potatoes
- 1 large carrot, finely sliced into rounds
- 2 large red onions, finely sliced into rings
- 1 bay leaf
- 4 sprigs thyme
- Peanut oil as needed

*For the vinaigrette:*

- Scant ¼ cup (50 ml) peanut oil (or other neutral oil)
- 1 tablespoon Dijon mustard
- A few sprigs flat-leaf parsley
- 1 tablespoon sherry vinegar

**PREPARATION**

A day ahead, place the herring fillets, carrot slices, onion rings, bay leaf, and thyme in a terrine dish, and pour in enough peanut oil to cover them. Chill for at least 24 hours.

The next day, prepare the mustard vinaigrette by combining all the ingredients.

Cook the potatoes (new potatoes need not be peeled) in boiling water, drain them, and cut them in half lengthwise.

When the potatoes are still warm, combine them with the vinaigrette. Arrange them on the plates, and top with the herring fillets. Garnish with the onion and carrot rings, and sprinkle with chopped parsley.

A dash of advice

This recipe is so easy that it barely deserves such a title. Yet each detail, each ingredient, plays an important role. The finest herrings are produced by J.C. David in Boulogne-sur-Mer, a port on the English Channel that has an annual herring festival, and the potatoes from Le Touquet have an AOC label (controlled designation of origin). Cook them at the last minute, and ensure that they are still warm when you serve them. A word of caution: nothing is more fatal to these potatoes than a sojourn in the refrigerator.

# Heirloom Vegetables

Imagine a bistro dish without vegetables. It would be like black-and-white TV or a silent movie. The vegetables are the words—the exclamations, even— that lively bistro cooking uses to expresses itself: lettuce, potatoes, tomatoes, zucchini, shallots, onions, beets, and carrots, to name but a few. They add color to your plate and make you smile just thinking of them. It was great chefs like Alain Ducasse, Michel Bras, and Alain Passard who were brave enough to give a starring role to the humble vegetable. They showed the way, and the bistros followed, embellishing what has become a celebration of diversity and seasonality. That's not to say that serving vegetables is a straightforward matter. Agriculture today seems to have lost its mind, spreading sulfates everywhere. The pastures are pasteurized; the carrots have droopy mops. The self-respecting bistro owner has to seek out the small farmers and market gardeners who respect the dignity of a humble onion without dousing it in insecticides every five minutes or hosing it down with bleach. Bistro owners are on a mission to protect vegetables and support sustainable farming systems. The bistro owner is an unlikely activist whose actions serve to preserve our farming heritage and ensure that our radishes retain their roots in the ground. And that is why a good dish of vegetables is now such a triumph: bistros are standing up for vegetables' rights.

*Vegetables are more than a mainstay of the bistro: they have become emblematic of an authentic style of cuisine that focuses on going back to its roots.*

# Calf's Liver
# with Green Asparagus

**SERVES 4**

- Four 8-oz. (220-g) thick slices calf's liver
- 1 lb. (500 g) green asparagus stalks

- 2 oz. (50 g) bacon
- 7 tablespoons (100 g) butter, divided

**PREPARATION**

Have your butcher cut four nice thick pieces (in French, they're known as *pavés*, or "slabs") of calf's liver. Select them from a liver that is small and light in color—the best, the ones we use in this recipe, come from the calves bred in France's Corrèze region.

Preheat the oven to 350°F (170°C). Slice the bacon as thinly as possible (if you have a meat slicer, now is the time to use it). Place the slices between two pieces of parchment paper, and set them on a baking tray. Cover with another baking tray to ensure that the slices of bacon remain flat. Dry them out in the oven for about 20 minutes.

Peel the raw asparagus—they need less peeling than white asparagus. Sauté them in half the butter over low heat for about 5 minutes. They must not change color, and they should retain their crunch.

In another pan, melt the remaining butter. When it is foaming, cook the liver slices for 2 to 3 minutes on each side on medium heat.

Arrange the green asparagus on the plates, and top them with a slice of calf's liver. Garnish with a slice of crisp bacon. If you wish, you can slice the liver on the diagonal, as you would for a duck *magret*.

# Sautéed Sweetbreads
# with Green Asparagus

**SERVES 4**

- Four 6-oz. (170-g) veal sweetbreads (make sure you ask for the heart sweetbreads, the finest part of the thymus gland and available at specialty meat markets)

- 1 lb. (500 g) green asparagus stalks
- 7 tablespoons (100 g) butter
- Salt and freshly ground pepper

**PREPARATION**

Using a sharp-tipped kitchen knife, carefully remove the fine membrane enclosing the sweetbreads. Allow half the butter to melt over high heat in a high-sided frying pan. When the butter is foaming, carefully place the sweetbreads in the pan and color them slightly. As soon as they are a nice light color, turn down the heat to low, and finish cooking them for about 5 to 7 minutes, turning them over regularly.

Peel the asparagus stalks. Sauté them in the remaining butter over low heat for about 5 minutes. They must not change color, and they should retain their crunch. Serve together.

*A dash of advice*

**Sweetbreads are offal with an extremely delicate taste. They pair marvelously with the magical wines produced by Côtes du Rhone winemaker Eric Pfifferling, particularly his 2009 Tavel.**

# Beef Cheeks with Wine Lees, Young Doubs Carrots, and Conchiglioni Pasta

**SERVES 4**

- Four ½-lb. (200-g) beef cheeks
- 6 ⅓ pints (3 l) wine lees or very strong, high-tannin red wine (13–14 percent alcohol)
- 2 calf's trotters, split in half
- 1 bouquet garni (thyme, bay leaves, and leek greens)
- 1 head garlic
- ⅕ oz. (5 g) juniper berries
- 2 oz. (50 g) pearl onions

- ⅓ oz. (10 g) fine bittersweet chocolate (optional)
- 2 teaspoons granulated sugar (optional)
- 3 ½ oz. (100 g) bacon
- ½ lb. (200 g) button mushrooms
- 4 large carrots
- 2 oz. (50 g) *conchiglioni* (shell-shaped pasta)
- Salt and freshly ground pepper
- 1 orange, preferably organic

**PREPARATION**

A day ahead, remove the outer membrane from the beef cheeks, and leave them to marinate with the bouquet garni, head of garlic, and juniper berries in the wine lees or red wine for 24 hours.

The next day, drain the cheeks into a bowl or directly into a pan, and flambé the wine lees or red wine for 5 minutes to remove the alcohol.

Brown the cheeks in a sauté pan until nicely colored; then season them with salt and pepper.

Place the cheeks, trotters, and lees or red wine in a large cooking pot.

Bring to a boil, and simmer gently for 3 to 3 ½ hours.

When the cheeks are done, remove them from the pot, and filter the sauce. Return the sauce to the pot, add the pearl onions, and reduce the sauce until it thickens.

If the sauce is too acidic, add the chocolate and sugar.

Cut the piece of bacon into bits, halve the mushrooms, and cook them in the sauce.

Adjust the seasoning.

Cut the carrots into large chunks, and cook them, either in stock or over steam. Cook the pasta. Add the carrots to the sauce, and return the meat to the pot. Lastly, add the *conchiglione*.

Just before serving, finely grate some orange zest over each plate.

*A dash of advice*

Full of finesse, this dish merits a slightly chilled red wine that is fruity and has a nice complexity, such as producer Jean Foillard's 2009 Fleurie.

# Roasted Pheasant au Jus with Buttered Green Cabbage and Bacon

**SERVES 4**

- A 2-lb. (1-kg) hen pheasant
- 1 onion
- 1 sprig thyme
- 1 bay leaf
- 1 teaspoon salt
- 1 teaspoon (5 g) freshly ground pepper

*For the buttered green cabbage:*

- 1 green cabbage
- 2 carrots
- 2 onions, chopped
- 2 ⅔ sticks (300 g) unsalted butter
- 7 oz. (200 g) bacon, diced
- ¾ teaspoon (3 g) freshly ground pepper

**PREPARATION**

Preheat the oven to 325°F (160°C).

Season the pheasant with the salt and pepper. Cut the onion into six pieces. Place the pheasant in an ovenproof dish with the cut onion, thyme, and bay leaf. Cook for 20 minutes.

Remove the pheasant from the oven, and transfer it to another dish. Pour in a half-glass of water to scrape out the juices; keep in a warm place.

To prepare the buttered cabbage: finely slice the cabbage using a mandolin. Finely dice the carrots and chop the onions.

Melt the butter in a sauté pan and then add the diced carrots and chopped onions. Fry gently, without allowing the garnish to color, for 5 to 6 minutes.

Add the green cabbage, season with pepper, and cook with the lid on over very low heat for 45 minutes, stirring regularly.

Halfway through the cooking, add the bacon bits, and adjust the seasoning. The bacon should be salty enough for no further salt to be required.

Finish cooking, maintaining the heat on low.

Carve the pheasant into four portions. In a serving dish, arrange the quartered pheasant on a bed of cabbage. Serve the cooking juices separately in a sauceboat.

A dash of advice

Pheasant or hen? The client considers what's on his plate to be pheasant, but as far as the hunter is concerned it's hen. The simple truth of the matter is that a hen pheasant is a female pheasant. If clients were only ever served pheasant it would often break their teeth! Hen pheasant, with its tender meat and slightly pronounced flavor, especially after it has been left to hang for a few days, calls for a wine that allies strength of terroir with elegance. A bottle of Côtes du Rousillon, such as a 2009 Les Glaneuses produced by Jean-François Nicq, seems ideal.

## L'Ami Jean

At L'Ami Jean (pages 72–75), food is served and eaten with relish. This is typical of the art of "bistronomy", exemplified by Yves Camdeborde's Le Comptoir. The owner of L'Ami Jean, Stéphane Jego, worked there before opening his own establishment in the seventh arrondissement. The menu seems to sing a familiar tune: hearty and straightforward, like its decor and clientele.

# The Wine

*With a neon sign like this, your taxi driver will know exactly where to drop you off. It is visible as far off as the Faidherbe-Chaligny and Faubourg Saint-Antoine crossroad, in the eleventh arrondissement in eastern Paris.*

A bistro without wine? It would be like … well, we'll spare you the traditional list of strawberries without cream, Christmas without snow, etc. Wine is a bistro's magical ingredient, that can take it to unsuspected heights. It is first encountered in a vertical position: at the bar. This is the difference between bistros and restaurants. You are presented with a wide range of easy-to-drink wines, simple wines you can order by the glass. They are wines that grease the wheels of conversation and whet the appetite. Candid, forthright wines: Gamay, Beaujolais, Morgon, Fleurie, and wines from the Loire Valley. Not too challenging, they carry you along and help you wind down. They are drunk not from the miniature *ballons* of yesteryear with their measly three fluid ounces but from generous, life-enhancing glasses that hold more than five fluid ounces (but that should never, oh never, be filled to the top). The wine must be allowed to take a deep breath—it's going to be leading you to your table after all.

Once at the table, the tone changes. You are handed the wine list. The wine list is an expression of the owner's personality, and each owner has his own personal geography. There has been a huge change in bistros' wine lists over the past few decades. There is no longer the humdrum distinction between Bordeaux and Burgundy. Now you'll only find wines from these regions decanted, as their prices have taken them into another dimension. Popular French

*Thanks to the humanistic vision of Bertrand Auboyneau, the Paul Bert's wine list is generously filled with authentic, often natural, handcrafted wines. These wines pair well with products rich in the goût de terroir—farm-made charcuterie and chunks of country bread, such as here at Le Grand Pan (facing page).*

wines have moved to the Loire Valley, with the Chinon, Bourgueil, Valançay, and Cheverny, and southward, with Côtes du Rhône, Languedoc-Roussillon, Collioure, and other southwestern wines. Today's wine list defies orthodoxy, and like the roots of the strong vines that pierce the earth, it tunnels its way toward out-of-the-way wines that have long been overlooked, wines that resist convention, and the interlopers—a pugnacious generation of table wines and *vins du pays*. It's in the bistros that you will encounter the guerillas, the rebels, and the experimental wines. The owner is there to introduce them and play the role of matchmaker as he gives you a rundown on their character. He talks for them, presenting their credentials to the public.

This is the bistro at its best, as long as it's careful not to make too much of a profit on the bottle and pad the bill. A restaurant will commonly charge between 3.5 and 8 times the buying price of a bottle. In a bistro worthy of this title, the margin may be as low as 1.8 for *grands crus*; it will rarely exceed 4. The bistro philosophy, shared by its clients, favors natural wines. These are produced in harmony with nature, without using pesticides on the vines, and without adding sulfates or yeast during vinification. The bistro serves wines that suit a clientele with an environmental conscience.

# Crisp Pig's Trotters with Tartar Sauce

**SERVES 6 TO 8**

- 8 pig's trotters
- 3 carrots
- 4 shallots
- 1 bunch tarragon

*For the aromatic garnish:*

- ¾ cup (200 ml) white wine
- 1 onion
- 1 stalk celery
- 2 cloves garlic
- 1 sprig thyme

- 2 bay leaves
- 1 carrot
- 1 clove

*To fry the trotters:*

- ½ cup (50 g) flour
- 3 eggs
- Scant ½ cup (2 oz./50 g) light-colored breadcrumbs
- Salt and freshly ground pepper
- Peanut oil (or other neutral oil) and butter, for frying

*For the tartar sauce:*

- 1 tablespoon Dijon mustard
- 2 egg yolks
- ¾ cup (200 ml) peanut oil (or other neutral oil)
- Salt and freshly ground pepper
- 1 bunch tarragon, finely chopped
- 2 shallots, finely chopped
- ⅓ oz. (10 g) salted capers, chopped

**PREPARATION**

A day ahead, place the trotters in a large pot, cover them with water, and cook with the aromatic garnish for about 3 hours.

When they are done, the flesh should come off very easily. Remove the trotters from the stock and carefully pick the meat off, taking care not to leave any small bones.

Take 4 cups (1 l) of the stock, and reduce it by half; then filter it.

Finely dice the carrots, and finely chop the shallots and tarragon. Add them to the reduced liquid with the meat of the trotters. Adjust the seasoning, and pour the mixture into a terrine. Chill for 24 hours.

The next day, cut the terrine into slices about ¾ in. (2 cm) thick. Dip the slices into the flour, then into a dish of beaten eggs, and lastly, into the breadcrumbs, coating them thoroughly.

Repeat the procedure for each slice. In French, this is known as "breading *à l'anglaise.*"

Season with salt and pepper.

To make the tartar sauce, prepare a mayonnaise. Mix the egg yolks, mustard, and salt and pepper in a bowl, and whisk in the oil, drop by drop, until it emulsifies. Incorporate the chopped tarragon, finely chopped shallots, and chopped capers.

You're almost done now. Gently heat a mixture of peanut oil and butter. Cook the slices of breaded pig's trotters for about 4 minutes on each side. They should turn golden and be nice and crisp.

**A dash of advice**

**If you think this recipe is too time-consuming, simply come and enjoy it at the Paul Bert.**

*The day's selection of life's little pleasures sitting in a wine cooler at the Paul Bert bar—to be enjoyed responsibly, of course.*

# Duck Breast with Morello Cherries and Roasted Baby Potatoes

**SERVES 4 TO 5**

- Four 12-oz. (350-g) duck breasts from fattened ducks
- 1 lb. (500 g) baby potatoes
- 1 ½ tablespoons (25 g) salted butter
- 3 shallots, chopped
- 2 garlic cloves, crushed
- 15 sprigs flat-leaf parsley, chopped
- 2 oz. (50 g) pitted morello cherries
- Pinch caster or granulated sugar

**PREPARATION**

Peel the potatoes, and cook them in a pan with the salted butter. When they are half-cooked, add the chopped shallots and crushed garlic to the pan. Scatter with the chopped parsley just before serving.

While the potatoes are cooking, first cook the duck breast with the fat side down in a nonstick pan without adding any additional fat. Cook for 7 to 8 minutes. Pour any fat that has dripped off into a bowl. Turn the breasts over, and cook for another 3 minutes. Leave them to rest on a plate.

Take the cherries, and toss them in the pan with a pinch of sugar. Leave them to color for 2 minutes, until the juice is a little syrupy.

To plate, place a nice crisp duck breast on each plate with the potatoes on one side and a line of cherry juice on the other. Top the breast with a few cherries.

Chill the duck fat from the pan, and reserve it for the next time you sauté potatoes (without parboiling them).

A dash
of advice

*Magret de canard*, duck breast from ducks fattened for their foie gras, is a strong-flavored red meat. It is produced in the southwest of France and deserves to be paired with a wine from this region. Côtes de Blaye winemaker Dominique Léandre-Chevalier's Le Queyroux strikes me as just perfect. The meat used here is from mallard ducks. The market for foie gras has exploded, and the demand for the meat has followed suit: it has the qualities of red meat but is nevertheless poultry.

Chevreny - Domaine ... | 2009 | 21
— Bourgogne Aligoté - S.M Bouzereau | 2009 | 21
— Chablis - Domaine Chevalier - J.L Chevalier | 2010 | 25
— Saint-Bris - Domaine Saint Prix - Busan | 2009 | 25
— Saint Véran - Joseph Drouhin | 2008 | 27
— Menetou Salon - Morogues - H. Pellé | 2007 | 28
— Pouilly Fumé "les Bonnes" - H. Pellé | 2009 | 32
— Cairanne - Domaine Richaud | 2006 | 33
— Beaujolais Blanc - Domaine Valette | 2004 | 33
— Bourgogne Chardonnay "les Châtaignres" H. Lamy | 2009 | 34
— Macon Chaintré - Domaine Valette - Vieilles Vignes | 2009 | 34
— Côte de Beaune "la grande Châtelaine" GIBOULOT | 2007 | 35
— Patrimonio - Grotte Disole | 2007 | 35
— Crozes Hermitage - Dard et Ribo | 2007 | 38
— Rully 1er Cru "le Mair Cadot" - V. Dureuil Janthial | 2004 | 38
— Saint Aubin "la Princée" - H. Lamy | 2006 | 45
— Chablis 1er Cru "Fourchaume" - B. Defaix |  |
— Sancerre ... - J.M Guillon |  |

## Bordeaux

— ... Côtes du Castillon - Marcillac | 2007 | 18
— ... de Bourg - Rollin Guénard | 2005 | 19
— Château Carcanieux - Cru Bourgeois ... | 2006 | 23
— Château Moulin - Canon Fronsac | 2006 | 25
— Château Calon - Montagne Saint Émilion | 2005 | 30
— Château le Auzejou - 1er Côte de Blaye | 2007 | 31
— Château la Commanderie - Saint Estèphe | 2007 | 36
— Closerie Mazeres - Pomerol | 2006 | 38
— Château Miurbeau - Pessac Léognan - C. Dubois | 2005 | 38
— Château Teynac - Saint Julien | 2002 | 44
— Château Rauzan Gassies - Grand Cru - Margaux | 2004 | 72

## Vins Rosé

— Touraine Noble Joué - Rousseau Frères | 2009 | 18
— Côte du Rhône - La Ferme St. Martin - Ventour | 2009 | 20
— L'Anglore - Tavel - Eric Pfifferling | 2008 | 22

## Les Bienfaits du Vin

| Maladie | Vin | Dose Journalière |
|---|---|---|
| Allergies | Médoc | 1 verre |
| Anémie | Graves | 4 verres |
| Artériosclérose | Muscadet | 4 verres |
| Bronchite | Bourgogne ou Bordeaux | 3 tasses |
| Constipation | Anjou blanc ou Vouvray | 4 verres |
| Affection des coronaires, Tuberculose | Champagne sec | 4 flûtes |
| Diarrhée | Beaujolais Nouveau | 4 verres |
| Fièvre | Champagne Sec | 1 bouteille |
| Cœur | Bourgogne, Santenay | 2 verres |
| Goutte | Sancerre, Pouilly Fumé | 4 verres |
| Hypertention | Alsace, Sancerre | 4 verres |
| Trouble de la ménopause | Saint-Emilion | 4 verres |
| Dépression Nerveuse | Médoc | 4 verres |
| Obésité | Bourgogne | 4 verres |
| Obésité importante | Rosé de Provence | 1 bouteille |
| Rhumatisme | Champagne | 4 flûtes |
| Amaigrissement anormal | Côte de Beaune | 4 verres |
| Paresse du foie | Champagne sec | 4 flûtes |

### The Marsangy

*The Marsangy is a typical Parisian bistro in the eastern part of the city. Here, the owner is hard at work in the kitchen but regularly comes into the dining area to take orders. The wine list is displayed on a sizeable chalkboard (pages 84–85) and complements the posters celebrating wine and other aperitifs (facing page).*

# Pollock Fillet with Sautéed Chanterelles

**SERVES 4**

- Four ½-lb. (250-g) thick pieces of pollock fillet, skin-on
- 14 oz. (400 g) small chanterelles
- 3 ½ tablespoons (50 g) butter
- 2 cloves garlic, crushed
- A few sprigs flat-leaf parsley, chopped
- Salt and freshly ground pepper
- Olive oil as needed

**PREPARATION**

Wash the chanterelles under running water, and dry them carefully using a clean cloth. Sauté them in a pan with the butter. After about 5 minutes, when they are done, add the garlic and chopped parsley.

In another pan, heat some olive oil over medium heat. Cook the fish fillets with their skin side down. After a few minutes, the fish should become slightly transparent, and the skin should be crisp.

Season with salt and pepper, and scatter with chopped parsley.

Serve the pollock fillets with the chanterelles.

# Breton Brill in a Beurre Blanc Sauce

**SERVES 4**

- Four ½-lb. (250-g) brill portions
- 7 tablespoons (100 g) butter

*For the beurre blanc sauce:*

- 2 ⅔ sticks (300 g) unsalted butter, diced
- 1 teaspoon sherry vinegar
- ¾ cup (200 ml) high-quality white wine
- Salt and freshly ground pepper

**PREPARATION**

First prepare the beurre blanc sauce. Pour the vinegar and white wine into a sauté pan, and leave to reduce until almost dry. Season with salt and pepper. Gradually whisk in the butter, and when it is incorporated, adjust the seasoning.

Heat the butter well in a pan, and cook the fish for 5 minutes on each side, depending on their thickness.

A dash of advice

- At the Paul Bert, it's the season that determines the side dish: green asparagus, small leeks, or wild mushrooms.
- Serve the sauce separately, so that the heat of the fish does not separate the beurre blanc.
- If you wish, add a few drops of lemon juice to the sauce.

# The Cheese Tray: A Fragrant Bouquet

You look at it with longing but, all too often, shake your head reluctantly, willing your calorie intake to stay below mind-boggling heights. Yet cheese is an integral part of the bistro. Remove the cheese from the bistro menu, and there would immediately be a chorus of complaints calling for its return. You can imagine deprived clients staging a hunger strike to demand its return. In some establishments, the cheese tray has been replaced by a cheese plate. In others, the tradition of this magical moment has been preserved. The most spectacular cheese tray of all is, without a doubt, at Yves Camdeborde's Le Comptoir. Like all true happiness, it's contagious. It's customary to offer at least six to eight cheeses, both soft and pressed (in years gone by, many bistros offered only pressed Cantal and Salers—they were easy to slice and kept well). Along with the cheese tray, good bread and butter must be served. When it comes to butter, opinions differ, although they coexist peacefully enough. The correct practice, though, is to offer salted butter to go with cheese; unsalted butter should be reserved for pastry making.

*The cheese tray doesn't have to be enormous,*
*but the selected cheeses should be ripe and ready to eat.*

# Blood Sausage, Apple, and Potato Parmentier

**SERVES 4 TO 6**

*For the mashed potatoes:*
- 2 lb. (1 kg) potatoes
- Scant ½ cup (100 ml) milk
- Scant ½ cup (100 ml) crème fraîche
- 7 tablespoons (100 g) unsalted butter

- Salt and freshly ground pepper
- Freshly grated nutmeg

*For the blood sausage layer:*
- 1 ⅓ lb. (600 g) blood sausage
- 2 teaspoons (10 g) butter
- 5 shallots, chopped
- 2 cloves garlic, chopped

- 15 sprigs flat-leaf parsley, chopped
- 2 Granny Smith apples
- 1 tablespoon plus 2 teaspoons (25 g) salted butter
- 1 ¼ teaspoons (5 g) sugar
- 1 oz. (25 g) light breadcrumbs

**PREPARATION**

First prepare the mashed potatoes. Cook them in boiling salted water, and mash them with a potato ricer or food mill. Using a spatula, stir in the milk, crème fraîche, and butter. Season with salt and pepper, and add the nutmeg (run the nutmeg over the grater about 3 times).

To prepare the blood sausage layer: melt the butter in a sauté pan. Add the chopped shallots and garlic, and cook over low heat without allowing them to brown.

Remove all the skin from the blood sausage, and place it in the sauté pan. Leave to cook for 5 minutes over low heat, mixing the ingredients. Remove from the heat, and add the chopped parsley.

Peel and core the Granny Smith apples, and cut each one into eight pieces. Sauté them in the salted butter with the sugar, leaving the pieces to cook for 2 minutes on each side. Remove them from the pan, and reduce the butter and sugar until a very light caramel forms.

Using four pastry rings, with a 4-in. (10-cm) diameter and height of 2 in. (5 cm), assemble the Parmentiers as follows: a layer of mashed potatoes, a layer of blood sausage, and lastly, another layer of mashed potatoes. Sprinkle with breadcrumbs.

Just before serving, place them under the broiler for 5 minutes, keeping a careful eye on the temperature and their color. Then top each one with a few pieces of apple and a spoonful of salted butter caramel. Serve with a generous helping of green salad.

A dash of advice

This is a real rough-and-ready bistro dish, and like all rough-and-ready guys, it doesn't give a hoot what anyone says about it. So it's just as comfortable being served with a nice lively, easy-drinking red wine, like iconoclastic and inspired winemaker Thierry Puzelat's pinot noir, as with Dard et Ribo's white Saint-Joseph. In the latter case, the dish becomes truly Parisian, served at the bar as an early lunch.

## Le Verre Volé

Le Verre Volé began as
a cute little store crammed
with remarkable wines
(pages 94–97) where
snacks were served for
customers to nibble
on as they tasted
the outstanding selection.
It has recently been
reinvented as a bistro,
serving authentic and
innovative cuisine.

# The Servers

*Particle accelerators*

W hat defines a bistro? A counter, an owner, and a chef? Limiting the definition to this trio would be too simplistic to describe an entire universe. A bistro comprises much more. The clientele, for example. No clients, and the bistro is like a singer without an audience—dismally depressing. Also missing are the waiters and waitresses. There are places where the owner does it all, but he doesn't look good. In fact, he's exhausted … and the clients eventually tire of waiting. The waiters and waitresses are the sinews of the war, the fuel, and the spark—they keep the motor running. Without them, the bistro wouldn't function; the clients would hotfoot it away; and we'd all be in hot water. Waiters act as go-betweens for the chef and owner. They bring the plates and remove them. They take care of all the details: drying glasses; serving wine; cutting bread; filling butter dishes; checking that the mustard pots are full; dusting the benches; removing the salt, pepper, and bread when it's time for dessert; bringing the steak knives; filling the water jugs; and serving the coffee as ordered.

If a bistro is a success, it's also due to the waitstaff (but don't tell that to the chef or the owner). If they are cheerful, savvy, and happy to be where they are, then—and only then—can the clients sit back and relax. You can't overestimate just how important this aspect is to the bistro experience. Gloomy, badly treated waiters are indicative of the rest of the establishment's state,

*Laetitia, at the Paul Bert, represents a new generation of waitstaff. It's servers' personal touch, warmth, and humor that convey the soul of the bistro. Taking an order becomes a real conversation, full of warmth and friendliness. This is what transforms a client into a regular.*

*At the Quedubon
(literally, "only good things,"
page 101), and (above,
left to right) at L'Abordage,
Le Verre Volé, the Repaire
de Cartouche, and
the Paul Bert, the service
counts just as much
as what's being served.*

right down to the vegetables that are badly chosen and carelessly stocked. Look closely, and you will see a clear correlation between the welcome you receive as you cross the threshold of a bistro and the quality of its crème caramel. If it's working well, you'll see no discord in the dance of the servers. They are there to oil the cogs, keep the clients loyal, help them choose their food and wine, and anticipate their needs—and whims. You'd like a pear-free *poire Belle Hélène*? But of course. You want your French fries fried to a crisp? No problem. They are like community police or chaplains spreading the good word. A good waitstaff finds ways to sidestep the constraints imposed by the owner and obtain special privileges, like extra French fries. They give a perfect theater performance, never overacting (as you might see in a brasserie), but weaving their way through the dining hall as proudly as tango dancers. They are the stars of this urban choreography, and they know it. You shouldn't be surprised to see them using their wide white aprons like bullfighters to make toreador-like passes. They usher the guests in warmly, and the audience, thrilled to be there, almost bursts into applause.

# Hard-Boiled Eggs with Truffled Mayonnaise

**SERVES 4**
- 4 eggs
- ⅕ oz. (5 g) black *melanosporum* truffles for garnish, or other black truffles

*For the mayonnaise:*
- 2 egg yolks

- ⅕ oz. (5 g) black *melanosporum* truffles
- 1 generous tablespoon Dijon mustard
- 6 ½ tablespoons (100 ml) grape-seed oil
- Salt and freshly ground pepper

**PREPARATION**

Two to three days ahead (if possible), store the eggs for this recipe in an airtight container with a few whole truffles. Just before serving, prepare the mayonnaise using a whisk if you're feeling energetic, or else a food processor (see page 81). Finely chop ⅕ oz. (5 g) truffles, and incorporate them into the mayonnaise.

Place the four eggs in gently simmering water for roughly 10 minutes, depending on their size. Working under cold running water, remove their shells, and cut the eggs in half lengthwise.

Place two halves on each plate with a generous spoonful of truffled mayonnaise. Place a slice of truffle on each egg half.

The water should be gently simmering because if it is too hot, the egg will cook too quickly, and the outer layer of the yolk will turn a greenish color and give off an odor of hydrogen sulfide. In short, your dish will smell of rotten eggs. So, instead of "hard-boiling" them, you should "hard-cook" them.

A dash of advice

# Fried Eggs with Black Truffles

**SERVES 4**
- 8 eggs
- ⅓ oz. (10 g) *melanosporum* truffles (or other black truffles)
- Scant cup (200 ml) cream, preferably heavy or double

*For the garnish:*
- ⅔ oz. (20 g) *melanosporum* truffles
- Salt and freshly ground pepper

**PREPARATION**

Two to three days ahead (if possible), place the eggs in an airtight container with some whole truffles.

A day ahead, cut the ⅓ oz. (10 g) truffles into small pieces, and stir them into the cream. Just before serving, simmer the cream very gently for 15 to 20 minutes.

Fry the eggs, and arrange them on the plates, two per person. Pour 3 tablespoons of truffled cream over the eggs, and garnish with the truffles you have set aside. If possible, use a truffle shaver to slice them. Season with salt and pepper.

A dash of advice

- For the aroma of the truffles to penetrate the eggs and cream, we recommend the method given here, so do remember to plan ahead.
- Take care to shave the truffle slices at the very last minute, so that they are still slightly crisp when served.

# Fattened Hen in Jura Vin Jaune and Homemade Mashed Potatoes

**SERVES 4**

- A 4 ½-lb. (2.2-kg) fattened hen
- About 3–4 pints (1 ½–2 l) chicken stock, or enough to cover the hen (for homemade stock, see *A dash of advice*, page 168)
- 4 shallots, chopped
- 1 tablespoon (15 g) butter

- ¾ cup (200 ml) heavy or double cream, 45 percent butterfat
- Scant ½ cup (100 ml) Jura *vin jaune*
- Salt and freshly ground pepper

*For the mashed potatoes:*
- 2 lb. (1 kg) potatoes
- ¾ cup (200 ml) whole milk
- ¾ cup (200 ml) whipping cream, 30–35 percent butterfat
- 3 ½ tablespoons (50 g) butter
- Salt and freshly ground pepper
- Freshly grated nutmeg

**PREPARATION**

Poach the hen gently in chicken stock, simmering it over low heat for 20 minutes. If you don't have a chicken carcass to make your initial chicken stock, use a good-quality stock cube.

Remove the hen from the stock, reserving the liquid, drain it, and complete the cooking in a 325°F (160°C) oven for 1 hour 30 minutes.

Carefully remove the skin, and cut the hen into four portions. Sauté the chopped shallots gently in the butter until they are translucent. Then stir in a scant ½ cup (100 ml) of the chicken stock and the thick cream. Cook over low heat to reduce until thick. Strain the sauce through a *chinois* or fine-mesh sieve, and return it to the pot with the *vin jaune*. Reheat it, and allow it to boil for just 1 minute. Season with salt and pepper.

To prepare the mashed potatoes, cook the potatoes in boiling salted water. Use a potato ricer or food mill to mash them. With a spatula, stir in the milk, cream, and butter. Season with salt, pepper, and a little freshly grated nutmeg. Serve the hen with some of the sauce spooned over it and two spoonfuls of mashed potatoes per plate.

You can use the hen carcass and skin to make an excellent stock—simply cover with water, and cook them together for about 15 minutes. Serve it hot with some large pearl tapioca and a few drops of lemon juice, or freeze it to use as a base the next time you make this recipe.

A dash
of advice

It's impossible not to mention Pierre Overnoy when the subject of *vin jaune* comes up. This winemaker is the forefather of today's natural wine artisans, the one who invented it all. In order to be able to express the full qualities of his amazing red wines and *vins jaunes*, you have to have drunk them. You have to have spoken to winemakers like Antoine Arena in Patrimonio, Thierry Puzelat in the Loire Valley, and so many others, to understand how meeting Pierre Overnoy completely transformed their way of thinking and of making wine.

# Give Us Our Daily Bread!

It may seem like a minor detail, but you can tell a lot from the bread you're served. You can gauge a bistro by the contents of the breadbasket, the way it is presented, served, and—most of all—its quality. Bread should smell good; it should be crusty; it should have personality. Good bread calls out for butter and whets your appetite. There is nothing more dreary than bread with no substance or smell—a dull bread that has nothing to say for itself. Even worse is factory-made bread, so washed-out, it's lifeless. Bread is the area code of a bistro: it tells you where it's at. It's the overture, announcing its freshness and honesty. Baguette should only be served at lunchtime. Any later, and it will lose its morning freshness and crust: the crumb will turn stale, and the baguette will have become a mere banality. Country bread like that made by Poujauran is more promising; it's sure to give momentum to a meal. Mushy bread will set the tone for a disappointing dinner—as will the absence of bread. The best is spirited bread, even if it is so tasty it rivals what's on your plate and attempts to outwit your meal with its goodness and flavor. And bread is at its best when we commit the ultimate (but not-so-deadly) sin at the table: using it to wipe off our plate. Bread is delicious when heated or toasted. Then it's like incense during Mass; a meal acquires biblical significance with the sharing of wine and bread. You are no longer at the table but back at the creation of the world.

*You may prefer a baguette to a country loaf, but there is no such thing as a good bistro that doesn't serve good bread. If it's fragrant and crusty, it's a sign of good things to follow.*

# Mi-Cuit Foie Gras Terrine with Stewed Kumquats

**SERVES 10**

When preparing the foie gras terrine, it's preferable to weigh the seasoning, as the amounts of salt and pepper are calculated proportionately to the weight of the foie gras.

- 3 ⅓ lb. (1.5 kg) foie gras
- 3 teaspoons plus scant ½ teaspoon (⅔ oz./18 g) salt

- ⅙ oz. (5 g) finely ground black pepper
- Scant ½ teaspoon (2 g) freshly grated nutmeg

- 1 lb. (500 g) kumquats
- 2 oz. (50 g) freshly grated ginger
- 4 sugar lumps
- 1 ½ oz. (40 g) pine nuts, divided

**PREPARATION**

Two days, or at least 36 hours ahead, make the foie gras terrine as follows.

Prepare the foie gras by removing the central vein. Handle it as delicately and as little as possible, and try to keep it whole, or as whole as possible.

Place the foie gras on a baking sheet and season it evenly all over. Leave it to rest for about 1 hour in the refrigerator. Preheat the oven to 150°F (65°C), and cook the foie gras, still on the baking sheet, for about 20 minutes. It should be warm, not hot, and glisten slightly (this is because of the fat it has given off).

Transfer the foie gras to a terrine. Cover it, preferably with plastic wrap, and press it with a weight placed firmly over it. After about 10 minutes, transfer the terrine to the refrigerator, still covered and weighted down, for at least 36 hours.

Prepare the stewed kumquats: wash them, and cut them in half. Place them in a saucepan with about 1 cup (250 ml) water, the grated ginger, and the sugar. Leave to stew gently for about 30 minutes. When they are nicely softened, add 1 oz. (30 g) pine nuts, transfer them to a jar, leave to cool, and set aside in the refrigerator.

Serve slices of the foie gras with a spoonful of stewed kumquats, and scatter the remaining pine nuts over the kumquats.

**A dash of advice**

Foie gras is one of those musts of bistro cooking. It is served hot in slices, cold in terrines, in salads, on toast, and shaved over lentil salad. Adepts of fusion food and molecular gastronomy make it crème brûlée-style or in iced flakes. Yves Camdeborde once served me extraordinary foie gras in a *cromesquis* (a small fried croquette with a liquid center) when he owned La Régalade. The secret to making a good dish with foie gras is—as always—the quality of the product. It must be fresh, pale, just veering towards a straw yellow, as silky as a baby's skin, soft to the touch without being squashy, and sold wrapped in paper, not vacuum-packed. Then you have to remove the veins as gently as possible, and then…well, everyone has his or her own recipe. So get to work, and *bon appétit!*

## L'Abordage

*Walk into L'Abordage*
*(pages 112–115) near the*
*Saint-Lazare train station,*
*and you're certain to say,*
*"Now this is what I call a real*
*bistro." The decor, the style,*
*the entrecôtes, and*
*the traditional andouillette*
*all speak of an authentic,*
*traditional establishment.*
*The owner, too, is true to type,*
*and Bernard Fontenille*
*knows what it takes*
*to keep his guests happy.*

Entrée du Jour 10€
Asperges sauce Loris

Plat du Jour 14€
- Rôti de Bœuf
  P. de Terre Maxim's
- Tartare de Bœuf préparé 18€
- Gigot d'agneau de lait
  Ratatouille 17€

Poisson du Jour 17€
- Pavé de Bar rôti aux Herbes
  Petits Légumes
- Tartare de Saumon
  Tabsulé

# Paris–Brest

**MAKES 8 INDIVIDUAL CAKES**

*For the butter cream:*
- 4 cups (1 l) milk
- 12 eggs
- 1 ¼ cups (9 oz./250 g) sugar
- 1 ⅔ cups (6 oz./170 g) all-purpose flour
- 9 sticks (2 ¼ lb./1 kg) butter, cubed
- 1 ¾ lb. (850 g) praline paste, available at specialty stores or online, at room temperature
- 1 ¼ cups (300 ml) whipping cream, 30–35 percent butterfat

*For the* choux *pastry:*
- ½ cup (125 ml) milk
- ½ cup (125 ml) water
- 7 tablespoons (3 ½ oz./100 g) butter
- 2 tablespoons (1 oz./25 g) granulated sugar
- 1 scant teaspoon (4 g) salt
- 1 ¼ cups (4 ½ oz./125 g) all-purpose flour
- 4 eggs
- A handful of slivered almonds

**PREPARATION**

Prepare the butter cream a day ahead.

Bring the milk to a boil. In a mixing bowl, whisk the eggs and sugar together until the mixture is thick and pale. Stir in the flour, mix well, and pour the boiling milk over the mixture, stirring as you do so. Return the mixture to the stove, and simmer, stirring constantly, until it is thick (the consistency should be that of pastry cream). Leave to cool a little; then gradually stir in the cubed butter. Mix well. Gradually stir in the praline and mix through. Chill for at least 12 hours.

To prepare the *choux* pastry, add the milk, water, salt, and sugar to a pan and bring to a boil. Pour in the flour, mix well, and simmer gently, stirring all the while, until the dough pulls away from the sides of the pan.

Preheat the oven to 350°F (180°C).

Remove the pan from the heat, and mix in the eggs, one by one, stirring well each time.

Spoon the dough into a pastry bag, and pipe out a 4-in. (10-cm) diameter circle of *choux* pastry onto a baking sheet. Pipe out another circle on top that is just slightly smaller. Repeat the procedure seven times to make eight cakes. Scatter the tops with slivered almonds, and bake for 30 minutes. Turn the oven down to 300°F (150°C), and bake for another 10 minutes, until the cakes turn a nice golden color.

Just before serving, whip the cream with an electric beater, and fold it into the butter cream.

Spoon the butter cream into a pastry bag.

Cut each cake in half horizontally, and pipe the cream out onto the lower half. Replace the top part, and dust it with confectioners' sugar.

A dash of advice

This pastry has a history. It was created in 1910 by a Monsieur Louis Durand, a pastry chef in Maisons-Laffitte, to the west of Paris, to celebrate the famous Paris–Brest–Paris bicycle race that crossed his town. He decided to make a cake in the shape of a bicycle wheel, comprised of two circles of *choux* pastry filled with a praline-based butter cream. We owe the introduction of this dessert at the Paul Bert entirely to my son Thomas, who learned how to make it in the kitchen of Gérard Besson, a famous chef with two Michelin stars, at his restaurant on the rue du Coq Héron in Paris. Today, this signature dessert at the Paul Bert is found on the menu of many bistros, but one of the best—if not the best—is made by Jacques Génin, pastry chef at La Chocolaterie in the Marais district of Paris.

# The Table

*"Dinner is served!"*

When you sit down at a bistro, the performance has already started, even before the appetizers appear. You may not even have detected that the stage is already set and the props ready; all you've registered are the rumblings of hunger in your belly. The action is ready to unfold along with the napkins. Napkins say a lot about the ambition of a bistro and its degree of distinction. All too often the napkin is made of poor-quality cloth that doesn't absorb a thing or even paper that disappoints by its ungenerous nature and its roughness when we dab our mouths. The latter is simply not up to the task and quite inadequate; it is no longer in its role. What we want, what we really dream of, is a wide, white, well-starched napkin that that we can spread out on our lap like a picnic blanket. A generous napkin is a poem in its own right. It protects the chests of gentlemen like a Roman shield and the legs of ladies when too much skin is showing or the temperature drops. Some people even fold it like a Japanese obi. A promising start to a culinary encounter, a good napkin is like a sail unfurled in anticipation of a culinary voyage.

The art of dining at a bistro may seem rudimentary; it can be almost biblical in its simplicity. The plates are round and white, like the halos of angels, and solid, like one's faith in good cooking. Nothing could be more serious than a bistro plate. It has to be strong to support and display the chef's creativity. The plate is the blank canvas of the bistro. The soul of the place will

*The moment has arrived. Along with the lighting, stage, and actors, the table is set for a much anticipated (last) supper. In a matter of minutes, the food will make a dramatic entrance. Each meal will be slightly different, and one never knows exactly how it will end—it's all part of the magic of dining out.*

*Whether to leave the table bare or cover it with a tablecloth is a matter for debate: each bistro follows its own lead, be it for a relaxed midday spread or the more formal evening meal. Above, left to right: Tables at L'Ami Jean and at the Quedubon are left completely bare, while at the Gorgeon, they are fully covered. Page 122: At Philou, a cautious compromise is reached.*

be inscribed upon it. The silverware is the supporting cast: it's heavy, easy to hold, and good for gesturing when the conversation becomes animated. There are other elements essential to any bistro table worthy of the name. The salt should have attitude. The pepper mill should be properly filled; ground pepper would be a dead giveaway to the establishment's status as also-ran. The table should also proudly bear a pitcher of cool water that is replenished regularly. Last but not least—a breadbasket and a carafe of wine. When all these vital props are in place, it's time to order from the menu or the chalkboard. The show is about to begin. Make sure you're comfortably seated; the curtain is about to unveil your meal.

Pavé de Cabillaud, épinards tièdes aux couteaux
Coquilles St Jacques rôties, purée de céleri rave (+4)
Joue de Boeuf, blettes fondantes
Poulet fermier rôti, grenailles et champignons
Carré de Porc rôti, endives
Rognon de Veau, petits légumes

Baba au rhum
Gelée de litchi, crème de thé
Fondue au chocolat, fruits et choux
Pomme rôtie, glace caramel
Parfait au Café

Chinon, Les Ro
Fleurie, Christ
Côtes-du-Rhône, lie
Vin de Pays de l'Ard
Morgon, Marcel
Alsace, Pinot No
Bandol, Dom
Vacqueyras, Lop
Saint Emilion g
Vin de Pays de l'Ard
Beaumes de Venise
MORGON, MARCEL

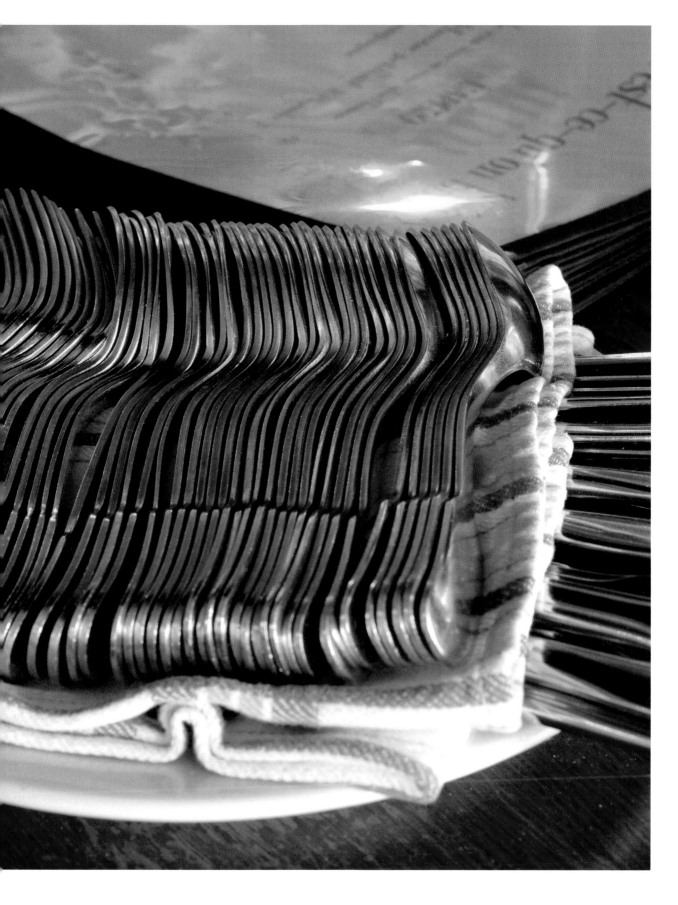

# Porcini Omelet

**SERVES 4**

- 12 oz. (320 g) porcini (allow 3 oz./80 g per person)
- 1 clove garlic

- 5 ½ tablespoons (3 oz./80 g) butter
- 12 eggs
- 4 teaspoons crème fraîche

- 2 tablespoons (10 g) finely chopped flat-leaf parsley
- Salt and freshly ground pepper

**PREPARATION**

Brush the porcini under cold running water, and dry them thoroughly.

Chop the garlic. Cut the porcini into medium-sized pieces, and sauté them in the butter with the chopped garlic for 5 to 6 minutes until a nice golden color.

Season with salt and pepper.

Whisk the eggs and cream together lightly—the mixture should not be bubbly—and stir in the chopped parsley. Pour the mixture over the porcini, and cook the omelet to desired consistency.

# Tongue Salad with Tarragon-Scented New Potatoes

**SERVES 4**

- 1 veal tongue
- 1 lb. (500 g) new potatoes, preferably *rattes* (Touquet variety) or other fingerling potatoes
- 1 red onion
- 1 bunch tarragon, chopped

*For the aromatic garnish:*

- 1 onion
- 1 clove
- 1 carrot
- 1 stalk celery
- 1 sprig thyme
- 1 bay leaf
- Peppercorns and salt

*For the vinaigrette:*

- Scant ½ cup (100 ml) peanut oil (or other neutral oil)
- 1 teaspoon sherry vinegar
- 1 teaspoon Dijon mustard
- 2 shallots, finely chopped
- Salt and freshly ground pepper

**PREPARATION**

Place the tongue in about 3 times its volume of water with the aromatic garnish, and bring to a gentle simmer.

Cook gently for about 2 hours 30 minutes.

When it is done, remove the outer membrane, and leave it to cool.

Cook the potatoes in salted water, and peel them.

Dice the tongue and potatoes.

Prepare the vinaigrette—mix all the ingredients thoroughly.

In a salad bowl, combine the diced tongue, potatoes, and vinaigrette.

Add the chopped tarragon leaves and finely chopped red onion, and serve.

A dash of advice

- When you prepare potatoes for a salad, it's essential to cook them just before you serve them, so they don't need to be refrigerated.
- For a vinaigrette, especially one you'll be using for a green salad, add 2 tablespoons of cooking juices from a roast, or even better, from a roast chicken, at the last minute. Alternatively, add an anchovy fillet: soak a Collioure anchovy (or other fine variety) in water to eliminate some of the salt, and mash it up.

# Sole Meunière with Lemon-Buttered Steamed Potatoes

**SERVES 4**

- Four 10–14-oz. (300–400-g) very fresh, line-caught soles
- 1 ¾ lb. (800 g) new potatoes
- ½ cup (1 ¾ oz./50 g) all-purpose flour
- 15 sprigs parsley
- 3 tablespoons (40 g) salted butter
- 2 tablespoons (30 g) unsalted butter
- Juice of 1 lemon

**PREPARATION**

Peel and steam the potatoes. Chop the parsley.

Peel the skin off the soles, or ask your fish seller to do so.

Spread the flour out in a dish, and dip both sides of the soles into it.

Heat the salted butter in a pan over high heat, and cook the soles for 2 to 3 minutes on each side until they are a lovely golden color. Transfer the soles to a dish or onto plates.

Melt the unsalted butter, and add the lemon juice to it. Leave for 1 minute before pouring into a sauceboat.

Sprinkle the potatoes with the chopped parsley, and spoon the lemon butter over them. Serve the potatoes with the soles.

# Entrecôte with Béarnaise Sauce and French Fries

**SERVES 4**

- Four 10-oz. (300-g) nice thick entrecôtes
- 2 lb. (1 kg) potatoes, cut into fries

*For the Béarnaise sauce:*

- 1 cup (250 ml) white wine
- Scant ½ cup minus 1 ½ tablespoons (100 ml) wine vinegar
- ⅓ oz. (10 g) crushed pepper
- 1 bunch tarragon, chopped
- 4 shallots, finely chopped
- 2 teaspoons (5 g) kosher salt
- 2 egg yolks
- 1 cup (250 g) melted butter
- 1 tablespoon plus 1 teaspoon (20 ml) water

**PREPARATION**

I'm confident that with your culinary talents, you are more than capable of cooking the entrecôtes and making the French fries. There's just one secret I'd like to share with you: put a little butter in your pan, and sear the meat well when you begin to cook it; then lower the heat. This will give you nicely browned entrecôtes with a hint of the grill. There's nothing worse than grey meat that hasn't been properly seared.

As far as the French fries are concerned, I'm sure you don't need my advice.

To make the Béarnaise sauce: place the white wine, vinegar, pepper, tarragon, shallots, and salt in a saucepan, and cook gently until the sauce thickens. Process or blend.

Add 2 egg yolks to the mixture, and whisk it like a sabayon over low heat. Once the sauce has thickened, stir in the melted butter little by little, as well as the water, stirring constantly.

*A dash of advice*

- Always serve the Béarnaise on the side, in a sauceboat.
- I'd like to remind you of the Paul Bert's motto when it comes to all red meat: "We serve red meat blue, rare, or badly cooked!"

# L'Écailler du Bistrot: The Call of the Open Sea

The success of a bistro often springs from an unexpected source. It could be a truly wonderful cheese tray, an aria-singing owner, or the biting wit of a waiter who has the room rolling. At the Paul Bert, it's the air of the Atlantic that has transformed a bistro hitherto anchored in classic tradition. When Gwenaëlle Cadoret, wife of Bertrand Auboyneau, opened L'Écailler du Bistrot just next door, the two eateries attracted eager clients in droves. While the Paul Bert went its jolly way, L'Écailler du Bistrot took a fresher, subtler direction. It's fun to compare the clientele of the two places in the evening. Although L'Écailler du Bistrot is far from being a formal or lofty establishment, it offers a taste of the very essence of Brittany, a region of strong, silent types. You can't shell a crab while you're howling with laughter. You need to be concentrated, hypnotically riveted on your task. The flesh of sole and the fascinating cavities of sea urchins are matter for different appetites and a different type of enjoyment. Here, a meditative spirit reigns; appetites are more delicate and focused. Gwenaëlle guides her establishment with a firm hand on the tiller.

*Adjacent to the Paul Bert is L'Écailler du Bistrot, boasting a catch sourced directly from Gwenaëlle's legendary Breton family, the Cadorets.*

## L'Écailler du Bistrot

A few years after opening
the Paul Bert, Bertrand Auboyneau
and Gwenaëlle Cadoret
decided to open another bistro,
one specializing in seafood.
They maintained the same decor
and introduced a nautical theme,
elegantly combining vintage
Breton bric-a-brac, ceramics,
and woodwork with marine
paraphernalia.
Each bistro has a distinct feel
and ambience; its own manifesto:
sedate and refined at L'Écailler
du Bistrot (pages 130–133),
exuberant and lively
at the Paul Bert.

# Roasted Figs with Tahitian Vanilla Ice Cream

**SERVES 4**

*For the ice cream:*

- 2 cups (½ l) whole milk
- ⅓ cup (2 oz./60 g) granulated sugar
- 1 Tahitian vanilla bean
- 8 egg yolks

*For the roasted figs:*

- 16 ripe figs
- 1 tablespoon plus 2 teaspoons (25 g) salted butter
- Scant ½ cup (100 ml) Corsican honey, or other flavorful honey

*Special equipment needed:*

- A Pacojet or ice-cream maker

**PREPARATION**

To make the ice cream, first prepare a basic custard (see the recipe for *Île Flottant*, page 188), carefully scraping out the seeds from the vanilla bean and mixing them with the milk, in which you should leave the whole bean. Leave to infuse for several hours in the refrigerator, and then prepare the custard.

Prepare your ice-cream maker or, better still, use a Pacojet, and pour the custard into it, following the manufacturer's instructions. You will need approximately 1 pint (½ l) of ice cream.

Preheat the oven to 350°F (180°C). Cut off the stems of the figs, and make a cross-shaped incision, about ⅓ in. (1 cm), on each side. Arrange the figs in an ovenproof dish, and top each one with a pat of butter. Spoon the honey over them, and bake for 10 minutes.

Place four hot figs in each dessert or soup plate, and in the center, serve a generous scoop of ice cream.

# Crêpes Suzette

**MAKES 15 TO 20 CRÊPES**

*For the crêpe batter:*

- 2 ½ cups (9 oz./250 g) all-purpose flour
- ¼ cup (1 ¾ oz./50 g) granulated sugar
- 4 eggs
- Heaped ½ teaspoon (3 g) salt
- Scant ¼ cup (50 g) melted butter
- 2 cups (500 ml) milk

*For the Suzette sauce:*

- 2 cups (500 ml) fresh orange juice
- 1 tablespoon (½ oz./12 g) sugar
- 4 tablespoons (60 g) butter
- Scant ½ cup (100 ml) Grand Marnier

**PREPARATION**

To make the crêpe batter, combine all the ingredients in a mixing bowl, and leave to rest for 1 hour in the refrigerator. Pour the batter out thinly in a well-heated nonstick crêpe pan (you don't need to grease it, but if you do, do so very lightly because there is melted butter already in the batter), and cook on both sides.

To prepare the Suzette sauce: combine the orange juice, sugar, and butter in a saucepan, and reduce over low heat until the mixture thickens.

Fold the crêpes into quarters; pour the sauce over them; and flambé with Grand Marnier.

*The desserts at the Paul Bert are so tempting, so delectable, that you almost want to begin your meal with one.*

# The Decor

*The backdrop to taste*

H ere's another French paradox: if the food is good, the decor seems spectacular. If the food is disappointing, the decor is filed away as iffy and the service spotty. It's only logical. If you are lucky, and the cuisine is brilliant, everything seems beautiful, charming, endearing. You'll love the crackled vase and opaline light shade. The bench covered in worn leatherette will seem redolent of the romance of past eras rather than simply shabby. Bistro decor is like traveling back in time to a golden age. There will be exposed brick walls, vintage posters, and enamel signage. All of these elements contribute to the enjoyment of the food; they are an extension of the owner's character and taste. Some collect books; others collect old wine posters. Some owners are more secretive, impassive, or rough-hewn. At their establishments, you'll find plates made of the same stern stuff. Look carefully, and you will see a familiar theme running from the door to the lamps, from the copper to the damask tablecloths. Then you can seek out the original state of the dining room: old tiling, molded ceilings, worn wooden tables, ancient chairs. They all transmit the same timeless message of enduring, reassuring solidity that can be relied upon to carry you effortlessly through your evening.

*At Le Comptoir, on the Left Bank, a little corner tucked away with subtle lighting creates the mood for a night to remember.*

*As you eat, your appreciative
gaze wanders from
one detail to another,
deriving pleasure from
the harmony between
the surroundings
and the food, as shown
here (above, left
to right) at Le Verre Volé,
Le Comptoir, the Gorgeon,
and L'Abordage (facing page).*

The decor never lies. You will hardly ever see stunning decor showcasing mediocre food, unless it's one of those sham places where the smiles are forced and the provenance of the veal chop and carrots is obscure. The decor can't be dissociated from its origins and take you for a ride. And that's why we are so confident when we open the door. The bistro is disarmingly naïve, putting the most timid appetites at ease. The decor of the bistro is like a quaint dialect, somewhat out of date, like words in sepia that reassure us and set our bellies rumbling.

# Green Asparagus, Parmesan Shavings, and Lardo di Colonnata with Sicilian Olive Oil

**SERVES 4**

- 2 bunches green asparagus
- 1 piece *lardo di Colonnata* (very fine Tuscan pork fat, available at gourmet stores)
- 1 piece aged Parmesan cheese, preferably Parmigiano-Reggiano, *Vacche Rosse* variety
- Sicilian olive oil
- Freshly ground pepper

**PREPARATION**

Peel the asparagus, shaving off the minimum amount of outer fibers, and cook them in boiling salted water. Drain them, and dry with a clean cloth.

Arrange the asparagus on a plate. Slice the *lardo di Colonnata* as finely as possible. If you have a meat slicer, set it to its thinnest setting, so that the pork fat slices are translucent.

Arrange the slices of pork fat over the asparagus, and add the Parmesan shavings on top. Drizzle the asparagus tips with olive oil, and season with freshly ground black pepper.

# Green Bean Salad with Aged Parmesan

**SERVES 4**

- ½ lb. (200 g) French green beans
- Scant ½ cup (100 ml) Greek or Sicilian olive oil
- 3 tablespoons (40 ml) sherry vinegar
- 6 shallots, chopped
- ⅔ oz. (20 g) pine nuts
- 3 oz. (100 g) cooked foie gras
- 5 oz. (150 g) aged Parmesan
- Salt and freshly ground pepper

**PREPARATION**

Cook the green beans in boiling salted water until they are al dente—it's important that they retain their crunch. To stop the cooking process, have a bowl of ice water ready when you remove them from the heat, and plunge them straight into this. This will ensure they remain green, and they will cool completely.

Pour the oil and vinegar into a mixing bowl, and season. Combine with the green beans and the chopped shallots. Toast the pine nuts in a pan, without adding any fat, for 2 minutes, stirring as they heat.

Cut the foie gras into thin slices, and finely shave the Parmesan.

Form a mound of green beans on each plate, combining them with half the Parmesan shavings and all the pine nuts. Arrange the sliced foie gras on top, and sprinkle with the remaining Parmesan shavings.

**A dash of advice**

If you put the foie gras in the freezer for 30 minutes before slicing, your task will be much easier. Use a swivel-blade vegetable peeler to ensure fine slices.

# Skate-and-Bell-Pepper Terrine with Dill-Scented Cream

**SERVES 4 TO 6**

- 4 ½ lb. (2 kg) skate wings
- 5 red bell peppers
- 5 green peppers

*For the court bouillon:*
- 2 cups (½ liter) water
- 2 cups (½ liter) white wine
- 1 carrot, cut into pieces
- 1 onion

- Greens of 3 leeks
- 1 bay leaf
- 2 teaspoons (10 g) salt
- 6 peppercorns
- 6 sheets (12 g) gelatin sheets (available online or at specialty stores)
- 1 tablespoon clear aspic

*For the dill-scented cream:*
- Scant ½ cup (100 ml) heavy or double cream
- 1 bunch dill, chopped
- Juice of ½ lemon
- Scant ½ teaspoon (2 g) salt
- 1 teaspoon (2 g) freshly ground pepper

**PREPARATION**

A day ahead, cut the peppers in half lengthwise, and remove the ribs and seeds. Place them in an ovenproof dish, and cook for about 20 minutes at 350°F (170°C).

When the skin has scorched, remove them from the oven, and wrap them in aluminum foil. Leave to rest until they are cool enough for you to handle, then remove the skins, being careful not to break them into too many pieces. Place them in a dish, and chill.

Prepare a court bouillon using the water, white wine, carrot pieces, onion, leek greens, salt, pepper, and bay leaf. Bring to a boil, and leave to simmer for 10 minutes. Remove all the aromatic ingredients and vegetables using a skimmer, and leave the court bouillon still simmering. Poach the skate wings in the bouillon for 3 to 6 minutes, depending on their thickness. Remove them carefully with a slotted spoon or skimmer, and arrange them, nice and flat, on a plate. Remove the flesh from the bones.

Next, prepare the jelly to hold the terrine together. Filter the court bouillon, and reduce it by three-fourths. While it is reducing, soften the gelatin sheets in lukewarm water. When they have softened, wring out the excess water, and incorporate them into the reduced court bouillon with the spoonful of clear aspic.

Adjust the seasoning.

Take an 8-in. (20-cm) long terrine, and line it with plastic wrap, making sure that it overhangs the mold enough to cover the top of the terrine afterwards.

Alternate layers of bell pepper and flaked skate, pouring a ladleful of liquid jelly between each layer.

Cover the terrine with the plastic wrap, and chill for 24 hours.

To prepare the dill-scented cream: combine the cream, chopped dill, lemon juice, salt, and pepper.

Just before serving, carefully turn the terrine out of the mold. Cut slices just under ½ in. (1 cm) thick; arrange them on plates; and serve with a dollop of cream.

*A dash of advice*

Fish and wine constitute an endless topic for debate. For decades, the diktat was clear: only white wine could be served with fish—period. Gradually, though, both customs and tastes evolved. Today, it's not unusual for us to serve a nice peppery red Pineau d'Aunis from Romain Guiberteau with oysters, or a red Cheverny from Hervé Villemade with a dish like pollock fillet with sautéed chanterelles.

# The Bistro Chair

The bistro chair is lighthearted, while the bistro bench (made of leatherette) is stoic and unmoving; a mere backdrop, it is there to catch the blows. According to Slavik, the famous bistro decorator, the success of a restaurant depends on the width and height of its benches. Absentminded brasserie clients have been known to nod off on a bench … only to find themselves on the floor. This couldn't possibly happen with a bistro chair, a symbol of salt-of-the-earth people, and a far cry from the pompous chairs of pretentious restaurants. The bistro chair is nifty and nimble, punctuating the dining space. It takes just a flick of the wrist to spin it. It is multipurpose: it can be straddled and stacked; it can be sent flying and even crack skulls. The original bistro chair was designed in 1859 in Michael Thonet's workshop in Boppard am Rhein, Germany. This ingenious inventor devised a process for bending solid wood into curved shapes, and it was the Thonet prototype number 14 that shot to success. The whole world then made knock-offs of his design, producing chairs that would support the world's most illustrious posteriors. Another version of the Thonet chair, with woven rattan, can be found lining terraces on sunny days. Today, bistros feature a variety of models, but they all share a stackable and sturdy wooden structure.

*This inviting chair awaits your company for the length of a meal.
Allow yourself to relax into its comfortable embrace as you anticipate
the pleasures of the evening.*

### Le Comptoir

Le Comptoir (pages 146–149),
near Odéon in the sixth
arrondissement, has become
a temple of Parisian
"bistronomy" thanks to its
good-humored and talented
chef, Yves Camdeborde, and to
the ambience, evening menu,
brasserie dishes on the weekend,
and lunch menu. The dining area
is always crammed, and the line
of eager diners-in-waiting
trails beyond the doors.

# Rum Babas, Savarin-Style

**SERVES 10 TO 12, DEPENDING ON THE SIZE OF THE MOLDS**

- 2 ½ cups (9 oz./250 g) all-purpose flour
- 2 tablespoons (25 g) sugar
- 1 teaspoon (4 g) salt
- 1 egg
- Scant ½ cup (100 g) melted browned butter
- ½ oz. (16 g) fresh yeast
- ½ cup (125 ml) milk

*For the rum syrup:*
- ¾ cup (200 ml) high-quality rum
- 1 orange, preferably organic
- 1 vanilla bean
- 1 lime, preferably organic
- 4 cups (1 l) water
- 2 ⅔ cups (500 g) sugar

*For the Chantilly cream:*
- 1 cup (250 ml) whipping cream, 30–35 percent butterfat
- 2 tablespoons (25 g) granulated sugar
- A few vanilla seeds

*Special equipment needed:*
- Savarin molds

**PREPARATION**

A day ahead, prepare the baba cakes.

In a large mixing bowl, combine the flour, sugar, and salt.

Incorporate the egg and melted butter.

In a smaller bowl, dissolve the yeast in the milk.

Add the milk and yeast to the bowl with the dry ingredients, egg, and butter. Then move the mixing bowl near a heat source (a wall heater or radiator, for example) for about 20 minutes, so that the dough can rise. It should more than double in volume.

Preheat the oven to 350°F (170°C).

Divide the dough among individual savarin molds. Bake for about 20 minutes, until golden brown, and then turn them out of the molds. Leave to dry for 24 hours.

The next day, begin by making the rum syrup. Quarter the orange, slit the vanilla bean lengthwise, and grate the lime. Combine the rum, water, sugar, orange quarters, vanilla bean, and lime zest in a saucepan. Bring it to a boil, and leave to simmer gently for 10 minutes.

Pour the hot syrup over the babas, and feel free to add another dash of rum.

And since we said, "savarin-style," we can't forego the Chantilly cream! Combine the cream, sugar, and vanilla, and whisk together with an electric beater. When the Chantilly reaches the right consistency, dollop a little into the center of each baba.

**A dash of advice**

Let's start at the very beginning. To make a *baba au rhum*, the essential ingredient is … well, rum. The balance of the dessert depends on your dosage. If it's too strong, it will overpower the sweetness of the sugar. If it's too mild, the sugar will outweigh the alcohol. If it's too strongly flavored, it becomes invasive. At our restaurant, we serve a sizeable *baba au rhum*, one that is often shared among friends. With its Chantilly cream, Tahitian vanilla, lime, sugar, and of course the famous rum, it's a child's dessert with grown-up panache.

*Mold used for casting silverware (Le Comptoir).*

# The Clients

*Unpredictable beings*

We can understand, to a certain extent, what led academics to petition for the French gastronomic meal to be added to UNESCO's List of Intangible Cultural Heritage, but we can't help but wonder whether the applicants slipped in a line or two about an unpredictable commodity: the clients. When it comes to clients, France has a dazzling array of bad characters. They constitute explosive material that can't be easily exported—except in the form of tourists.

It's no exaggeration. Just stand at the bar in any bistro, and you will be able to gauge the seriousness of the situation. You're bound to spot one or more clients looking downhearted, sullen, morose, or annoyed. Some of them manage to display the whole range of gloomy emotions from bleakness to wretchedness. Those who enter laughing and jolly are few and far between, and their demeanor inevitably raises the suspicion that they have been enjoying their predinner drinks.

The work of the owner and his team involves putting each and every client at ease, reassuring them, tucking them in. You want another seat, chair, or napkin? You would like to change your side dish and have new salt-and-pepper shakers brought to the table? No problem. Anything is possible: a crème caramel without caramel; an order of steak and French fries without the fries; or a club sandwich without bread, mayonnaise, or bacon. Managing all this requires stoicism and the love of one's job. French clients are unique creatures, and it is in this spirit that they must be welcomed. In theory, the customer is king, but there are

*What is a bistro without guests? A song without words, a film without music. The guest gives the cue for the show to begin. When the client arrives, the kitchen is set in motion, picking up momentum as the dining area fills. The saddest thing that can happen to a restaurant is for it to be empty. The chef is down at heart; the owner panics; fresh produce goes bad; and the bank manager grows impatient....*

*The guest helps shape the identity of a restaurant, like here (above, left to right) at the Quedubon, the Gorgeon, and the Baratin, an authentic thirty-seat bistro nestled at the edge of the twentieth arrondissement, and at Le Verre Volé (facing page).*

limits to the patience of a waiter, and that of the owner is worn thin even more quickly. The success of an evening at a bistro can often hinge on a single client. A grumpy person who complains nonstop can easily spread his mood to neighboring tables. The scene caused by one intransigent oddball over one slightly crushed garden pea will be detrimental to the general atmosphere. And this is why bistro owners are so attentive to the diners, keeping them under constant, close surveillance. Just one cantankerous person who loses his or her patience or explodes can quickly ruin the ambience. An owner needs many attributes, not the least of which is his ability to sooth and pacify. Often, however, this is not enough. Table safety precautions are needed for lovers and those who are getting ready to no longer be lovers. The former can't sit still, mistaking the tablecloth for a sheet and the bread for a pillow. The latter are as sharp as the steak knives. Both categories are assigned to faraway tables (in Siberia, so to speak), so if they boil over, or their passion upsets the laws of gravity and decency, the owner will have time to neutralize them and send them gently on their way to resolve their issues in private. But in case you were wondering: there are also happy clients. Some of them come from far-flung places. They have dropped their bags off at their hotel and have come to pay homage to their first Parisian bistro. When they arrive, the world feels right again: the bistro is no longer a refuge for crosspatches but once again fulfills its vocation of a welcoming inn. When this happens, the atmosphere is as happy as it is meant to be.

# Suckling-Pig Head Cheese

**SERVES 4 TO 6**

- 4 heads of suckling pig
- 10 ½ pints (5 l) water
- 1 lb. (450 g) sodium nitrite (0.6% NaNO$_2$)
- ¼ cup (50 g) granulated sugar

*For the aromatic garnish:*

- 2 carrots
- 2 onions
- 2 cloves
- Greens of 1 leek
- 1 stalk celery
- 3 bay leaves
- 3 sprigs thyme
- 1 ¾ teaspoons (5 g) black peppercorns
- 3 calf's trotters

*For the broth:*

- ¾ cup (200 ml) vinegar
- 8 shallots
- 2 cloves garlic
- 1 bunch flat-leaf parsley
- 1 bunch tarragon

**PREPARATION**

Two days ahead, prepare the brine by combining the water, sodium nitrite, and sugar.

Leave the heads to soak in the brine for 24 hours, and then rinse them under running water. Place them in a pot, completely covered with water, and cook with the aromatic garnish for about 2 hours 30 minutes over low heat. When they are done, take a small knife, and detach all the flesh (both the fatty and lean parts), and place it all in a bowl. Filter half the cooking liquid through a *chinois* and reduce it by three-fourths.

Adjust the seasoning.

A day ahead, chop the shallots, garlic, parsley, and tarragon. Bring the vinegar to a boil, and pour it over the chopped shallots and garlic. Add the chopped herbs. Combine the reduced cooking liquid with the vinegar, herbs, and the flesh removed from the heads. Arrange it all in a terrine, and chill for at least 24 hours. For a well-balanced terrine, alternate the lean meat with the fattier parts and those that have a little gristle.

Serve the terrine with a mustardy, tarragon-scented vinaigrette or a slightly sweet wine-lees mustard.

**A dash of advice**

This recipe takes us to the epicenter of the bistro, to its very heart, where we are rubbing elbows with the other clients, glass in hand. This head cheese—also known as "brawn"—is, along with herring and potato salad and pork muzzle with vinaigrette, a must-have bistro appetizer.

# Savory Escargot-and-Sweetbread Tartlets

**SERVES 4**

*For the puff pastry:*

- 4 sheets puff pastry (to save time, buy the best ready-made puff pastry you can find; if you're living in France, order it from your favorite baker)
- 1 egg yolk mixed with 1 tablespoon water

*For the garnish:*

- 20 snails
- 5 oz. (150 g) high-quality, raw sweetbreads, in ¾-in. (2-cm) cubes
- 2 shallots, chopped
- 6 button mushrooms, thinly sliced
- Scant ¼ cup (50 ml) white wine
- Scant ¼ cup (100 ml) heavy or double cream
- Salt and freshly ground pepper
- Freshly ground nutmeg

**PREPARATION**

Roll out the puff pastry onto a baking sheet and cut it into eight 2 ½-in. (5-cm) squares.

Take half of the squares, and cut out 1 ¼-in. (3-cm) squares from their centers.

Dip a pastry brush into water, and brush the full squares with it. Place a cut-out square over each full square. Chill.

Preheat the oven to 400°F (200°C). Brush the tops of the pastry squares with the mixture of egg yolk and water.

Bake for about 20 minutes, keeping an eye on them, until golden.

To prepare the garnish, gently sauté the chopped shallots for 5 minutes. Add the sliced mushrooms and diced sweetbreads. Deglaze the pan with white wine. Immediately add the cream and snails, and cook over low heat for another 5 minutes.

Season with salt and pepper, and grate a little fresh nutmeg over the mixture.

Fill the puff pastry squares, which should still be warm, with the garnish, and serve with a salad of fresh herbs.

A dash of advice

This revisited *feuilleté* is redolent of *bouchées de la reine*, vol-au-vent, and other recipes that our grandmothers and bistro chefs have regaled us with. These recipes were concocted to make use of offal, leftovers, and cheap cuts of meat, and they were scrumptious!

TABLE N° 8
COUVERTS 2
1 ASPERGE
1 cochon
TABLE N° 20 bis
COUVERTS 1
1 Asperge
1 Veau
TABLE N° 9
COUVERTS 4
3 cochon
TABLE N°
COUVERTS 2
48
TABLE N° 15
COUVERTS 2
49
2 Baba
TABLE N°
COUVERTS
4
1 Gigot
1 Saumon,
TABLE N°
COUVERTS
4
2 Gigot

# A Bistro Will Never Be Perfect

An underdone fillet of beef, a disappointing tartlet, a hair in the soup, a piece of plastic in the pâté, sand in the lamb's lettuce, lead shot in the game.... Even in the fanciest establishments, the unthinkable can happen. A mouse scuttles between the chairs, and a wasp hovers over the strawberry tart. Being in a temple to "bistronomy" is no guarantee that everything will be perfect, immaculate, and faultless. The bistro resembles life with all its blemishes and even illustrates that there is no such thing as unmitigated excellence. If a waiter spills sauce down the back of your neck, don't get too excited—it's just a reminder of the imperfections in this earthly world. The average bistro serves up to 150,000 dishes a day, which translates into 40,000 clients over 100,000 hours. Sooner or later, an accident will happen. What else can you expect? Don't think of it as a disaster; it's just life taking its course. Remember that the bistro is forbearing when you're in a mad mood, have left your wallet at home, or forgotten to cancel your reservation, so the next time your chicken wing is a little too droopy, your skate takes a slide, or your soufflé flops, try to be indulgent.

*Taking your order is a crucial moment in the unfolding of the evening's symphony at the bistro.*
*The sheets of paper hanging here, at the Paul Bert, are the score.*

## Le Grand Pan

*This bistro (pages 164–167)
could be in a village. The
entrance is wide, open to the
intersection, easily accessible—no
obstacles to traverse or hurdles
to jump on your way in. You are
warmly welcomed, as the shiny
copper bar twinkles its greeting.
Here are the newspapers; there
are the calendars and even a rugby
flag. If you look hard enough,
you will probably find the electricity
bills. Calm and tranquility reign
at Benoît Gauthier's Le Grand Pan.
The long table d'hôte dominates
the main dining room, wide and
rustic with its two benches. Clients
know that they will encounter
a friendliness that is not always
easy to find in Paris. What's on the
plate is superb: finest quality meats
like the cut of beef of the Blonde
d'Aquitaine breed, specially
selected by the famous butcher
Mauléon and grilled on the
plancha; an Ibaïona pork chop;
or a delicate pigeon.*

# Fillet of Beef with Sarawak Pepper

**SERVES 4**

- Four ¼-lb. (250-g) thick beef fillets
- 1 oz. (25 g) Sarawak peppercorns
- 5 tablespoons (75 g) butter
- Scant ½ cup (100 ml) high-quality Cognac
- 1 ⅔ cups (400 ml) heavy or double cream, 45 percent butterfat
- Salt

**PREPARATION**

Crush the peppercorns using a pestle and mortar, and roll the fillets in the crushed pepper to coat them.

Place the butter in a pan over high heat, and when it is foaming, sear the fillets on each side. Season with salt. Deglaze with the cognac, and flambé the contents of the pan.

Pour the cream into the pan, and continue cooking the meat to desired doneness. Remove it, and leave it to rest in a warm place. Leave the cream to cook until it reaches desired consistency.

# Roasted Pigeon on a Bed of Buttered Green Cabbage

**SERVES 4**

- Four ½-lb. (500-g) pigeons
- 1 green cabbage
- 3 onions
- 3 ½ sticks (400 g) butter, divided
- 2 oz. (50 g) bacon
- Scant ½ cup (100 ml) white wine
- Salt and freshly ground pepper

**PREPARATION**

Have your butcher prepare the pigeons, setting aside the livers and hearts.

Begin by preparing the buttered cabbage. Shred the cabbage with two of the onions, and sauté the slices in 3 sticks (350 g) of the butter. Add the bacon, and put the lid on the pot. Simmer over low heat for 30 to 40 minutes, until the cabbage is nicely softened.

Chop the remaining onion. Place the remaining butter (½ stick/50 g) in a cast-iron pot until it melts. Add the livers and heart and the remaining chopped onion. Cook for 3 minutes, and remove from the pot, reserving the cooking juices.

Preheat the oven to 350°F (180°C). Season the pigeons with salt and pepper, and place them in the pot. Cook them in the oven for about 15 minutes, depending on desired doneness. My preference is for rare pigeon meat, and if you like it rare, too, reduce the cooking time slightly. Allow about 10 minutes of cooking time for pigeons of the size specified here. Deglaze the pot with the white wine, and reduce it by two-thirds.

Coarsely chop the sautéed livers and hearts. When the sauce is reduced, add them to it just before serving. Season with salt and pepper. Arrange the buttered cabbage in the center of a plate. Serve the pigeon on its bed of cabbage, and spoon the sauce with the chopped livers and hearts over the meat.

Pigeon carcasses—as with all poultry— can be used for broth. First, remove the meat using a small knife to cut away the fillets and legs from the carcass, just as you would for a roast chicken. If the fillets are a little too rare for your liking, cook them again in a pan for 2 to 3 minutes. For the broth, place the carcasses in a saucepan and add 4 cups (1 l) water, a small bouquet garni, and salt and pepper. Simmer gently for 20 minutes. Remove the carcasses from the broth, filter it, and reduce it by half. Add a few herbs and 3 cubes of foie gras per person, and voilà: a delicious appetizer!

A dash of advice

# SPECIAL

## FILET DE BOEUF
## AU POIVRE
## 34€

accompagné de frites maison
et salade verte

servi bleu, saignant, ou mal cuit!!

# Tarte Tatin

**SERVES 4 TO 6**

- 2 lb. (1 kg) Golden Delicious apples

*For the pastry:*

- 2 ⅕ sticks (9 oz./250 g) butter
- 2 ½ cups (9 oz./250 g) all-purpose flour
- ¼ cup (1 ¾ oz./50 g) granulated sugar
- 1 teaspoon (4 g) salt

*For the caramel:*

- ¾ cup (200 ml) water
- 7 tablespoons (100 g) butter
- ¼ cup (1 ¾ oz./50 g) granulated sugar

*Special equipment needed:*

- An 8-in. (20-cm) cake pan

**PREPARATION**

Peel, core, and quarter the apples.

Place the ingredients for the caramel in a saucepan over medium heat until the liquid turns a light caramel color. Pour the caramel into the bottom of the cake pan.

Preheat the oven to 350°F (180°C). Arrange the apple quarters, thick-side down, evenly around the pan. Place the pan over low heat on the stove, and cook gently for 10 minutes. Finish cooking the apples in the oven for 15 minutes.

Remove them from the oven, and allow to cool.

To prepare the pastry: melt the butter. Combine the flour, sugar, and salt. Pour in the hot melted butter, and stir to mix. Roll the dough out to form a 12-in. (30-cm) circle. Transfer the dough to the cake pan, tucking the edges in (you may want to use a spoon to do this), so that the apple quarters are enclosed.

Turn the oven up to 400°F (200°C), and bake the tart for 10 minutes.

# My Grandmother's Chocolate Cake

**SERVES 6**

- 9 oz. (250 g) bittersweet chocolate, 70 percent cocoa
- 1 ¾ sticks (7 oz./200 g) butter, plus extra for greasing the pan
- 4 eggs
- 1 ¼ cups (9 oz./250 g) sugar

*Special equipment needed:*

- An 8-in. (20-cm) cake pan, 2 in. (5 cm) deep

**PREPARATION**

Preheat the oven to 350°F (180°C). Butter the cake pan well.

Melt the chocolate with the butter over a double boiler, or cautiously in a microwave oven.

Whisk the eggs with the sugar until the mixture is pale and thick.

Combine all the ingredients, and pour the batter into the cake pan.

Bake for 40 minutes, until the top is smooth and flat and a cake tester or knife tip comes out sticky from the center.

Leave to cool before turning out of the pan. This cake is not to be chilled.

## The Repaire de Cartouche

There are two entrances to Rodolphe
Paquin's restaurant on the boulevard
des Filles du Calvaire in the eleventh
arrondissement, each leading to
a very different dining area. But
the skilled cooking of the chef
is the same. With a robust wine
list to boot, the Repaire de Cartouche is
one of the best bistros in eastern Paris.

# The Ambience

*The bistro soundtrack:*
*A happy hubbub*

In the winter, the bistro terrace is a refuge for chronic smokers who huddle together against the cold like sparrows on a branch. Then, once spring arrives, the terrace becomes a prelude to the sun and summer vacation; an air of freedom flutters between the plumes of cigarette smoke and lightly-tanned faces; everything seems possible, and life is wonderful.

Nothing is more fragile than the ambience of an eating place. It's like the original soundtrack of a movie. The restaurant manager might be tempted to shout out, "Lights… Camera… Action!" when the evening gets underway, the moment when the ambience is set. The ambience might be loud and boisterous—this would be a brasserie. Myriad conversations, the clinking of cutlery, waiters overacting their roles, and barked-out orders all come together in a life-affirming babble. Then there is the soundtrack of the chic restaurant: sudden exclamations against a backdrop of constant murmuring, the clack of stiletto heels on wooden floorboards, a sound like cloth rustling or wings beating. Or perhaps you like the calm, understated concerto of the small discreet restaurant, like a fire burning in the fireplace, a contented purring, the sound of life flowing smoothly along. A general state of well-being resonates through the dining hall: a ladle dishing out sauce; a gentleman clearing his throat; a cork popping out of a bottle; spoons tinkling against coffee cups. It's all silky smooth and slow.

The ambience of a bistro is original and inimitable. It is forthright and sincere. At the beginning of the service, there is an expectant hush. It's like school before the bell rings. One by one, the players enter, so the improvised concert can begin. Naturally, there are conversations (they swell, resound, calm down, and start all over again); the waiters and waitresses interject

*If the reservation book could divulge the secret of a good bistro, a new one would open every day in Paris. The ambience is the result of a subtle interplay of personality and cuisine. A single bad-tempered patron or iffy dish is enough to upset this delicate balance.*

loudly, hollering out their orders and reminders. There is the clatter of cutlery clinking on the plates of a hastily reset table; the echoing of new arrivals' of footsteps on the tiled floors, laughter bouncing off the mirrored walls.

The noise level is representative of the concern for quality. There will be irascibility when a plate doesn't arrive promptly (*"Service!"* will resound like a castanet). The thundering voices may be a little disconcerting, but there is nothing more reassuring. Sometimes, clients talk too loudly, shouting at each other as though they were separated by a cornfield. But who cares? It's all part of the little annoyances specific to the bistro and what makes a bistro good, as well as what we reproach it for—it's too full; it's too lively; it's too good! Lastly, there is one essential thing that distinguishes a good bistro from a "sham" bistro. In the sham bistro, music is required because there is no soundtrack of well-being, conversation, or the pleasure of being together.

# Anchovy Fillets with Marinated Red Bell Peppers

**SERVES 4**

- 1 ⅓ lb. (600 g) very fresh anchovies
- 5 red bell peppers
- ⅓ oz. (20 g) Espelette pepper (a mild chili pepper from the Basque region of France)
- ¾ cup (200 ml) olive oil
- Salt and freshly ground pepper
- A drizzle of high-quality olive oil

**PREPARATION**

Prepare the marinated red bell peppers and anchovy fillets a day ahead.

Preheat the oven to 350°F (180°C).

Cut the bell peppers in half lengthwise, and carefully remove all the seeds. Place the pepper halves on a baking sheet, and cook for about 20 minutes. Remove them from the oven, and wrap them in aluminum foil until they have cooled enough for you to remove the skin easily.

Cut them into strips just under 1 in. (2 cm) wide. Season them with salt and pepper, and marinate them in the olive oil overnight in the refrigerator.

To prepare the anchovy fillets: remove the fillets from the central bone. Season with salt and pepper, and sprinkle with the Espelette pepper. Leave overnight in the refrigerator.

To serve, alternate slices of bell pepper with anchovy fillets on the plates. Drizzle with your very best olive oil.

Serve this dish with a thin slice of warm country toast spread with black olive tapenade.

A dash of advice

Anchovies—fresh, marinated, or fried—served with black or green olives and a glass of white wine are a must for *l'apéro*, the popular abbreviation for *apéritif*. This tiny migrating fish is found from Istanbul to Saint-Jean-de-Luz on the Atlantic coast of southwestern France. It has brought riches to the canning factories of Collioure (on the Mediterranean) and sown discord between Spain and France, who quarrel about the limits of their territorial seas. It's hard to imagine that this minute silvery fish with its blue reflections could stir up tempers to such an extent or be so highly coveted.

## Philou

*Philippe Damas has disappeared from the Square Trousseau near the Bastille, but we tracked him down in the tenth arrondissement, not far from the Canal Saint-Martin. Damas is a bistro lover who has transcribed his recipe for success at Philou with its cheerful atmosphere, warm welcome, pleasing decor, and most of all, a mouth-watering chalkboard menu. From corn soup and foie gras sautéed with figs to free-range roast chicken with baby potatoes and chanterelles or plaice with artichokes, the daily menu will overwhelm you with choices.*

# Hanger Steak with Marrow, Shallots, and Sautéed Potatoes

**SERVES 4**

- Four 7–8-oz. (200–250-g) hanger steaks or *onglets* (France)
- 4 pieces of marrowbone
- 2 cloves garlic
- A few sprigs flat-leaf parsley
- 1 ¾ lb. (800 g) potatoes
- 6 tablespoons (90 g) salted butter, divided
- 10 shallots, chopped
- Freshly ground pepper

**PREPARATION**

Cook the marrowbones in the oven at 325°F (160°C) for 15 minutes.

Chop the garlic and parsley. Finely slice the potatoes, just under $^1/_{16}$ in. (2 mm) thick. Heat 4 ½ tablespoons (70 g) butter, and sauté the potato slices in it. Add the chopped garlic and parsley when the potatoes are half-done.

Cook the shallots in the remaining butter until they are a light golden color.

To cook the hanger steaks, proceed as you would for a classic steak, but remember that this cut has long muscle fibers that cannot withstand cooking at a very high temperature—it causes the fibers to retract, making the meat hard.

When the meat has reached desired doneness, carefully remove the marrow from the bones. Cut it into small slices, about ⅓ in. (1 cm) thick.

Serve each steak on a plate with three or four slices of marrow and the shallots on top. Arrange the sautéed potatoes on the side.

A dash
of advice

- In France, hanger steak used to be considered offal and was sold by *tripiers*, along with tripe, liver, and kidneys. But today there are hardly any of these shops left, and their traditional produce is sold by butchers. Hanger steak has long muscle fibers and a pronounced taste. It must be cooked only briefly, so that the muscle fibers retain their juiciness.
- The trick for crisp sautéed potatoes is not to wash them once they have been sliced. Water would remove all their starch, and without it, they will not fry as well.
- This is a bistro dish *par excellence* and pairs well with a Côtes du Rhône, like a 2008 La Sagesse, produced by the Domaine Gramenon.

# Knife-Cut Steak Tartare

**SERVES 4**

- Four 1 ¾–2 ⅕-lb. (800 g–1-kg) beef fillets, fat removed
- 2 egg yolks
- 1 teaspoon Dijon mustard
- 1 bunch flat-leaf parsley, chopped
- 1 oz. (25 g) salted capers

- 2 grey shallots, finely chopped
- A drizzle of olive oil
- ½ teaspoon Tabasco sauce
- Salt and freshly ground pepper

**PREPARATION**

Dice the meat into ⅕-in. (5-mm) cubes.

Combine the egg yolks, mustard, parsley, capers, chopped shallots, oil, and Tabasco sauce.

Carefully stir in the diced beef.

Season with salt and pepper. Use a pastry ring to shape the mixture, but don't make it too compact, as this crushes the meat fibers.

**A dash of advice**

- What is essential here is to cut the beef into the right-sized cubes, as the meat must remain tender and retain its texture.
- For the most delicious finished product, choose ingredients of the finest quality for your tartare mixture.

# Panfried Langoustines with Seaweed Butter

**SERVES 4**

- 1 ⅓ lb. langoustines, preferably live
- 1 ⅓ sticks (160 g) seaweed butter

**PREPARATION**

Heat a frying pan well, and melt the seaweed butter. When the butter is foaming, add the langoustines, and fry them for 1 minute on each side.

Transfer to plates, and serve immediately.

## Desserts: The Cherry on Top

Desserts play a less than starring role in many bistros—it's not their style. They want to brandish their swords on savory ground, talk in terms of terrines, hanger steaks, and casseroles. Dessert, for them, is pure whimsy. The clients, satiated by the cheese course, no longer have room, and the bottle of wine has been emptied. So there goes dessert time—which is a shame because, more often than not, an establishment expresses its generosity through its desserts. Even a simple tart of the day, when made with love, can provide the final flourish to a meal. Then there are the veritable desserts, creamy and big-bottomed: the authentic rum baba, a Paris-Brest, strawberries with Chantilly cream, an old-fashioned chocolate mousse, gâteaux Saint-Honoré, and more. As you read this, the sweet richness of a memorable dessert or two has probably returned to your lips for a moment. The mission of the dessert is to carry the meal into another dimension, to hit a high point without a care for the dictates of diets. The happiness we find at the table often comes when we steal moments away from time and enjoy an escapade away from routine.

*Often by the time you get to dessert, your hunger is already satisfied. But you may still be tempted by a sweet temptation, such as the famous* cannelé *from Bordeaux.*

# Vanilla-Scented Île Flottant and Pink Pralines

**SERVES 6**

- A handful of pink pralines (candy-coated almonds whose coating is not caramelized)

*For the custard:*

- 4 cups (1 l) whole milk
- ¾ cup (5 ¼ oz./150 g) granulated sugar
- 18 egg yolks
- 1 Tahitian vanilla bean

*For the caramel:*

- ¼ cup (1 ¾ oz./50 g) granulated sugar
- Scant ½ cup (100 ml) water

*For the meringue:*

- 18 egg whites
- 1 cup (6 oz./200g) granulated sugar
- Pinch salt

**PREPARATION**

To prepare the custard, slit the vanilla bean lengthwise, and scrape the seeds out into the milk. Place the bean into a saucepan with the milk, and bring to a boil.

Whisk the egg yolks and sugar together.

Pour the boiling milk over the egg yolk mixture, stirring as you do so. Return the mixture to the stove, and cook over low heat, stirring constantly, until it thickens and coats the back of a spoon. As soon as the custard is ready, cool it as quickly as possible: to stop it from cooking any further, pour it into a bowl set in a larger bowl filled with ice water.

To prepare the caramel: heat the sugar and water together until they turn a light caramel color.

To prepare the meringue: preheat the oven to 350°F (180°C).

Begin beating the egg whites with the pinch of salt. Then, when they first begin to stiffen, add the sugar. When they form nice stiff peaks, shape them into six domes with a ladle. Pour the caramel into an ovenproof dish, and carefully place the shaped egg whites over it. Bake for 10 minutes.

While the meringues are baking, coarsely chop the pink pralines.

Use deep soup plates to serve this dessert. Pour 5 tablespoons of custard into each dish, scoop out a baked meringue covered with caramel, and float it, caramel-side up, in the custard. Scatter with the chopped pink pralines.

A few vanilla beans, a handful of pink pralines, and there you have it. But things are not always so simple. One evening at the Paul Bert, everything was going wrong. Christian Millau, a loyal friend, noted food critic, and ruthless gourmand, told us that the vanilla was tasteless. We didn't know what to do; we didn't know what to say. The chef tasted; I tasted … and we could only concede the point. As the saying goes: the devil is in the detail. We would try to do better next time, we promised. We ask our clients to be clement, for we are only artisans after all. We constantly call ourselves into question, and we take more heed of criticism than of compliments.

### The Gorgeon

*It really is a small world. Christophe Acker, the owner of this bistro (pages 190–193) in Boulogne-Billancourt, just west of Paris, used to work at the Paul Bert. So you'll find the same jovial reception and down-to-earth cooking: egg with mayonnaise, hanger steak, blood sausage and apple, an enormous entrecôte served with homemade French fries. The easy-to-drink wines are there, too—in short, you'll find everything that comprises the perfect bistro.*

# The Aromas

C an you imagine walking into a bistro with a clothespin on your nose? You would lose your bearings completely, for your nose is as important to you as your sight. Imagine, however, a sightless person entering such an establishment for the first time. What a feast of odors, smells, and fragrances he or she would find! A bistro has an olfactory profile, just like any restaurant, train station, or garage. Entering it is like lifting the lid of a cooking pot. A bistro's bouquet doesn't lie, although it does change during the course of the sittings. If you're lucky enough to come right at the start, you'll discover disarmingly clean smells: scents of wax polish, crisp tablecloths, and fresh ingredients wafting from the storage areas. The bouquet is already rounded, but it will evolve ceaselessly over the evening: from pâtés to stewed dishes to vanilla-scented pastries. A feast for the nose!

The bistro is a library of aromas that have been forgotten or are on the endangered list: the crumb of good bread, cheese *gougères*, Brie cheese, roasted and grilled meats, long-simmered stews, and the steam that wafts out of cast-iron pots. But beware the strong-smelling cabbage, the skate or langoustines that carry a whiff of ammoniac, and the game that is ... well, too gamey! Like any dish, this aromatic stew is fragile: its harmony has to be nursed from the beginning to the end of the cooking process. In this delicately balanced environment, anyone wearing too strong a scent can cause

*A bistro without any smell would be like a universe lacking a fundamental dimension or a person lacking a fifth sense. Its enticing aroma completes the dining experience.*

*Whether at L'Ami Jean, the Quedubon, or (yet again) the Paul Bert (above, left to right), the bouquet of a bistro is created by the wonderful alchemy of fresh products and simmering pots.*

an atmospheric disturbance. A perfume that is too strong or too musky may well put off the clients, not to mention the owner. Just imagine a wonderful white wine emerging from the dark of a cellar and clashing with the perfume of tuberose. The bowl of the wine glass will capture the scent and combine with the bouquet of the wine, imperceptibly disturbing it. The same is true of the food, whose fragility is more unexpected. Luckily, the no-smoking laws in restaurants have improved the sensorial dimension of the food beyond belief. Years ago, the dining area was weighed down with smoke, which was an inevitable part of a bistro's atmosphere. With its cloud of burning tobacco, saturated energy, and shared euphoria, the bistro of days of yore looked like an airship powered by its own grey whirls and curls.

Nowadays, things are different, but nevertheless, beware of the odor-free, personality-less bistro. The banality—its lack of harmony, even—is obvious for all to see. A cook who uses a microwave stands no chance of sending the fragrances of his creations into the dining area. There will be no enticing aromas. The establishment turns into a desert. The bouquet of a bistro, like the aura of a person, is one of the biggest clues to its character.

# Cuttlefish Sautéed with Raspberries, Verjus-Style

**SERVES 4**

- 1 lb. (500 g) small cuttlefish
- 3 oz. (80 g) raspberries
- Scant ½ cup olive oil, divided
- Salt and freshly ground pepper

**PREPARATION**

Rinse the cuttlefish quickly under cold running water, and dry them using a clean cloth.

Crush the raspberries with a fork, and set aside. Heat half the olive oil in a very large pan, and quickly sauté the cuttlefish in it, for 30 to 45 seconds.

Add the raspberries to the pan. Drizzle in the remaining olive oil just before serving.

- It's essential to use a large pan, so that the cuttlefish are evenly distributed in it. This will ensure that they are seared very quickly, without giving off any water.
- *Verjus* is a very old condiment made from green grapes; it was widely used in cooking during the Middle Ages. Here, we replace the grapes with raspberries.

# Kari Gosse-Scented Scallops on the Shell

**SERVES 4**

- 8 lb. (4 kg) scallops in their shells
- 2 ¼ sticks (250 g) salted butter
- ½ oz. (15 g) Kari Gosse (see below)

**PREPARATION**

Clean the scallops, taking care that they remain attached to their shells.

Preheat the oven to 375°F (190°C).

Soften the butter, and incorporate the Kari Gosse, mixing thoroughly.

Place a pat of seasoned butter in each scallop shell, and cook for 2 minutes in the oven.

Kari Gosse, inspired by Indian spices, is a spice mix made in Lorient, Brittany, dating from the time of the French East India Company. It can be found at certain specialized grocery stores and online. If needed, substitute it with a high-quality curry powder; the result, however, will not be quite the same.

## The Quedubon

*This bistro (pages 200–203) near the Parc des Buttes Chaumont in Paris holds all the playing cards. Gilles Bénard is an experienced bistro owner, having created the Ramulaud and then Les Zingots on rue du Faubourg Saint-Antoine. In the kitchen, his son Léo is always at work. Léo trained with Raquel at the Baratin and produces food of deceptively brilliant simplicity, like cod tart, pork chops with homemade mashed potatoes, and Basque terrines and charcuteries—all accompanied by his father's outstanding wine selection.*

# Monkfish with Green Asparagus

**SERVES 4**

- Four 7-oz. (200-g) monkfish tails
- 14 oz. (800 g) small green asparagus stalks
- 3 ½ tablespoons (50 ml) Greek or Sicilian olive oil plus 1 tablespoon to drizzle over the dish
- Salt and freshly ground pepper

**PREPARATION**

Peel the monkfish tails.

Trim, peel, and wash the asparagus.

Cook the asparagus in boiling salted water for 8 to 9 minutes. For the method we recommend, see page 21.

Heat the oil in a pan, and cook the monkfish tails for 1 minute 30 seconds on each side. Then drain them.

Arrange the asparagus on individual plates, and top with the monkfish tails. Drizzle with a little olive oil.

# Panfried Red Mullet with Tempura Vegetables

**SERVES 4**

- Eight 5–7-oz. (150–200-g) red mullet
- ½ cup (1 ¾ oz./50 g) all-purpose flour
- 3 ½ tablespoons (50 ml) olive oil
- 5 oz. (150 g) red bell pepper
- 5 oz. (150 g) green bell pepper
- 5 oz. (150 g) eggplant (aubergine)
- Salt and freshly ground pepper

*For the tempura:*
- 3 ¼ tablespoons (20 g) all-purpose flour
- 2 tablespoons (⅔ oz./20 g) cornstarch
- 1 egg
- 2 teaspoons (10 g) celery salt
- Scant ¼ cup (50 ml) sparkling water or soda water
- Scant ¼ cup (50 ml) beer
- ¾ cup (200 ml) peanut oil (or other neutral oil, but the taste will not be quite the same)

**PREPARATION**

To prepare the tempura, combine the flour and cornstarch in a round-bottomed mixing bowl. Make a well in the center and add the egg and celery salt. Whisk together, adding the sparkling water and beer. The consistency should be fairly thick (it should form a ribbon) but still liquid enough to pour. Set aside in the refrigerator until needed.

Dice the peppers and eggplant into 1 ¼-in. (3-cm) cubes. Season them with salt and pepper. Begin heating the peanut oil in a sauté pan. Dip the vegetable cubes into the tempura batter, and add them little by little to the pan. (We do this gradually so as not to lower the temperature of the oil too suddenly, and so that the cubes do not stick to one another.) When they are a nice golden color, remove the vegetables and drain them on paper towels.

Lightly dip the mullet into the flour, shaking off any excess. Pour the olive oil into a heated pan, and sear the mullet for 3 to 4 minutes, depending on their thickness.

**A dash of advice**

You'll know your tempura batter is well made if it swells when it is in the oil.

# Coffee: The Grand Finale

Dinner's over. It's the end of the meal, almost time to leave, when a steaming cup of coffee arrives with its creamy foam, the sign that the beans have been well ground and the water heated to the right temperature: the two secrets to a good cup of coffee. If coffee beans are ground too coarsely, the water from the machine filters through them too quickly, making the coffee watery; if the beans are ground too finely, and the water filters through too slowly, the coffee is bitter. If the water is too hot, it destroys the aromas, and if it's too cold, it can't extract them. Coffee is as complex as wine, and its quality and taste depend on its provenance and terroir (the aromas of Arabia, the humidity of South America, the strength and character of Africa), its variety (Arabica or Robusta), the way it's blended, the treatment used when it's harvested, and of course, the way it's roasted. All these factors are concentrated in the fragrances that waft up from the cup. Organic producers, fair-trade advocates, tycoons, and manufacturers share this important commodity, the price of which holds a powerful influence over the global economy. Drinking coffee is a voyage that transports us, like travelers of yesteryear, along the Spice Route, through former colonies. No gourmet will forego these few burning, bitter sips after a meal laden with savory and sweet, sometimes even overwhelming, sensations. Coffee opens the door for departure. It's the moment just before we leave our friends, kiss them goodbye, and decide where we'll spend the night…. It's the last stage in a journey and the very last aroma we savor before the bill brings us back to earth with a thump. And there it is: the bill sits in its little saucer; the waitress waits for it to be settled. And that's when I hear: "We'd like two more coffees, please."

*The bistro has its last word when coffee is served. If the final note of the score is out of tune, it will ruin the evening. Red IAPAR, an Arabica from Brazil, is the bean of choice at the Paul Bert.*

# Fromage Blanc Ice Cream

**SERVES 4**

- ½ lb. (250 g) farm-made *fromage blanc*
- ¼ cup (1 ¾ oz./50 g) granulated sugar

*Special equipment needed:*

- A Pacojet or ice-cream maker

**PREPARATION**

Whisk the two ingredients together. Pour the mixture into the Pacojet bowl or your ice-cream maker, and that's it! Just follow the manufacturer's directions.

A dash of advice

- A recipe does not have to be long; it has to be good. Enjoy this ice cream in the summer with berries, in the fall with chestnut cream or bittersweet chocolate shavings, and in the winter with fragrant honey, chopped hazelnuts, and cooked cinnamon-sprinkled apple quarters. In the spring, you can eat it by itself because that's when the milk in farm-made *fromage blanc* tastes the best. Children love it; so do adults.
- French *fromage blanc* is an unsalted, fresh dessert cheese with a very high water content. Thicker than yogurt, it is often served with fruit or fruit coulis in France. It is closely related to German *quark*; you can also use Greek yogurt as a substitute.

# The Simplest Apple Tart

**SERVES 4**

- 3 large Granny Smith apples
- 1 ⅓ sticks (5 ⅔ oz./160 g) butter
- 2 tablespoons plus 2 teaspoons (40 ml) water
- 2 tablespoons white sugar
- Pinch salt

- 3 cups (300 g) all-purpose flour
- 4 tablespoons (1 ¾ oz./50 g) light-brown sugar (*vergeoise blonde*, if possible)

*Special equipment needed:*

- A 12-in. (32-cm) pie dish

**PREPARATION**

Place the butter in a saucepan to melt. Add the water, sugar, and pinch of salt. Bring the mixture to a boil. Remove from the heat, and pour in the flour, mixing with a fork until thoroughly incorporated.

When the dough is cool enough to handle, spread it out evenly in the pie dish with your fingers.

Preheat the oven to 350°–400°F (180°–200°C), and cover the dough with a sheet of wax paper. Spread out pie weights evenly over the surface, and bake until the dough is a nice golden color.

Cut the apples into thin slices, and lay them evenly over the crust.

Sprinkle the apples slices with the light-brown sugar, and return the tart to the oven for a few minutes just before serving.

A dash of advice

I got this recipe from the well-known Michel Picquart, who used to own Chez Astier and Le Villaret, two quintessential Parisian bistros.

## Classic Parisian Bistros

We have tried to define the distinctive characteristics of the bistros selected for this book, yet they all add up to one essential principle: the enjoyment they provide. We set out to define the authentic bistro through its tangible elements, its esthetics, and its cuisine, but we know that both guests and gastronomy professionals have shifting requirements when it comes to their favorite haunts. So we have also tried to pinpoint the more abstract dimension of the iconic bistro, personified by its owner, its chef, and its clientele. This alchemy is as incomprehensible as love, yet it is the very essence of "bistronomy." A bistro is a place where birds of a feather flock together; it fulfils a need to come together with kindred spirits—others who identify, just like you, with the food, wine list, and offerings. Most of all—and this is perhaps wherein lies the secret of the bistro—there is the personal touch and the symbiotic relationship between staff and guests. It is theater where each guest plays his or her starring role. There is a feeling of belonging: the clients feel that they are participants, even stakeholders.

Friendship and generosity are the common denominators of the following establishments, which François Simon and I prize above all other eating places.

**The Paul Bert**
**18, rue Paul Bert**
**75011 Paris**
**Tel.: +33 (0)1 43 72 24 01**

All the photographs in this book were taken at the Paul Bert except those mentioned below.

**L'Écailler du Bistrot**
22, rue Paul Bert
75011 Paris
Tel.: +33 (0)1 43 72 76 77
*See pages*: 128, 130, 131, 132, 133.

**L'Abordage**
2, place Henri Bergson
75008 Paris
Tel.: +33 (0)1 45 22 15 49
*See pages*: 102, 112–113, 114, 115, 139, 174, 210 (bottom, left).

**L'Ami Jean**
27, rue Malar
75007 Paris
Tel.: +33 (0)1 47 05 86 89
*See pages*: 4 (top, left), 36, 72–73, 74, 75, 120, 194, 196, 212 (top, center).

**The Baratin**
3, rue Jouye Rouve
75020 Paris
Tel.: +33 (0)1 43 49 39 70
*See pages*: 14, 36, 50, 51, 156.

**Le Comptoir**
9, carrefour de l'Odéon
75006 Paris
Tel.: +33 (0)1 43 29 12 05 or
+33 (0)1 44 27 07 97
*See pages*: 136, 138, 146–147, 148, 149, 150, 210 (center, left).

**The Gorgeon**
42, avenue Victor Hugo
92100 Boulogne
Tel.: +33 (0)1 46 05 11 27
*See pages*: 120, 138, 156, 190–191, 192, 193.

**Le Grand Pan**
20, rue Rosenwald
75015 Paris
Tel.: +33 (0)1 42 50 02 50
*See pages*: 79, 164–165, 166, 167, 210 (top, left).

**The Marsangy**
73, avenue Parmentier
75011 Paris
Tel.: +33 (0)1 47 00 94 25
*See pages*: 4 (bottom, center), 36, 55, 84–85, 86, 87.

**Philou**
12, avenue Richerand
75010 Paris
Tel.: +33 (0)1 42 38 00 13
*See pages*: 122, 180–181, 210 (bottom, right).

**The Quedubon**
22, rue du Plateau
75019 Paris
Tel.: +33 (0)1 42 38 18 65
*See pages*: 4 (bottom, right), 101, 108, 118, 120, 144, 156, 176, 196, 200–201, 202, 203, 206, 210 (top, center and right), 212 (center, left).

**The Repaire de Cartouche**
8, boulevard des Filles du Calvaire
75011 Paris
Tel.: +33 (0)1 47 00 25 86
*See pages*: 102, 172, 173.

**Le Verre Volé**
67, rue de Lancry
75010 Paris
Tel.: +33 (0)1 48 03 17 34
*See pages*: 94, 95, 96–97, 102, 138, 157, 210 (center, right), 214.

**Le Villaret**
13, rue Ternaux
75011 Paris
Tel.: +33 (0)1 43 57 89 76
*See pages*: 42, 44, 45.

*Facing page, left to right from top left: Benoît Gauthier of Le Grand Pan, Gilles Bénard of the Quedubon, Bertrand Auboyneau, Bernard Fontenille of L'Abordage, and Philippe Damas of Philou.*

# The Paul Bert's Suppliers

The finest produce of French terroirs can be found in our kitchen and on our tables. We source them over the course of our wanderings in the countryside and in vineyards, often finding them through sheer serendipity. Attached as we are to quality and to farming methods that some would have us believe are obsolete, we treasure each and every one of our suppliers for their respect for nature and strong ties to their land. Our existence and the continuity of a certain lifestyle depend on people such as these producers, whose concerns go far beyond net profit. So that you can enjoy what we serve at the Paul Bert at your own table, I am happy to open my address book and share it with you here.

## WINE

**Antoine Arena**
Domaine Antoine Arena
20253 Patrimonio
Corsica
Tel.: +33 (0)4 95 37 08 27
www.antoine-arena.fr

**Michèle Aubery-Laurent**
Domaine Gramenon
26770 Montbrison-sur-Lez
Tel.: +33 (0)4 75 53 57 08

**René-Jean Dard and François Ribo**
Domaine Dard et Ribo
26600 Mercurol
Tel.: +33 (0)4 75 07 40 00

**Jean Foillard**
Domaine Foillard
69910 Villié-Morgon
Tel.: +33 (0)4 74 04 24 97

**Romain Guiberteau**
Domaine Guiberteau
49260 Saint-Just-sur-Dive
Tel.: +33 (0)2 41 38 78 94
www.domaineguiberteau.fr

**Lise and Bertrand Jousset**
Domaine Jousset
37270 Montlouis-sur-Loire
Tel.: +33 (0)2 47 50 70 33
www.domaine-jousset.fr

**Dominique Léandre-Chevalier**
Château Le Queyroux
33390 Anglade
Tel.: +33 (0)5 57 64 46 54
www.lhommecheval.com

**Agnès and René Mosse**
Domaine Mosse
49750 Saint-Lambert-du-Lattay
Tel.: +33 (0)2 41 66 52 88
www.domaine-mosse.com

**Jean-François Nicq**
Domaine des Foulards Rouges
66740 Montesquieu
Tel.: +33 (0)6 88 11 83 02
www.lesfoulardsrouges.over-blog.com

**Pierre Overnoy and GAEC Emmanuel Houillon**
Maison Pierre Overnoy-Emmanuel Houillon
39600 Pupillin
Tel.: +33 (0)3 84 66 24 27

**Eric Pfifferling**
Domaine de l'Anglore
30126 Tavel
Tel.: +33 (0)4 66 33 08 46

**Thierry Puzelat and Pierre-Olivier Bonhomme**
Domaine Puzelat-Bonhomme
41120 Les Montils
Tel.: +33 (0)2 54 44 05 06
www.puzelat.com

**Jean-Baptiste Senat**
Domaine Senat
11160 Trausse
Tel.: +33 (0)4 68 78 38 17
www.domaine-jeanbaptistesenat.fr

**Isabelle and Hervé Villemade**
Domaine du Moulin
41120 Cellettes
Tel.: +33 (0)2 54 70 41 76

## FOOD

**Annie Bertin**
*Organic fruit and vegetables available at the weekly Marché des Lices in Rennes.*
Blot
35140 Vendel
Tel.: +33 (0)2 99 97 63 58

**Jean-Yves Bordier**
*Artisanal butter.*
La Rivière
35530 Noyal-sur-Vilaine
Tel.: +33 (0)2 99 04 17 17
www.lebeurrebordier.com

**Manuel Borniambuc**
*Crème fraîche from Borniambuc is a work of art.*
27210 Fort-Moville
Tel.: +33 (0)2 32 57 83 85

**Boucherie du Rouillon**
*Wholesale meat supplier.*
102, avenue Henri Dunant
91200 Athis-Mons
Tel.: +33 (0)1 69 38 48 33

**Jean-Jacques Cadoret**
*A traditional Breton oyster farm.*
Établissement Cadoret
La Porte Neuve
29340 Riec-sur-Belon
Tel.: +33 (0)2 98 06 91 22
www.huitres-cadoret.com

**Poissonnerie Le Dundee**
*Authentic Breton seafood vendor.*
22, rue de la Marine
29730 Le Guilvinec
Tel.: +33 (0)2 98 58 10 23
www.laurentdaniel.fr

**J.C. David**
*Salted herring specialist.*
15 and 17, rue Georges Honoré
62200 Boulogne-sur-Mer
Tel.: +33 (0)3 21 87 38 31
www.jcdavid.fr

**Christophe Dru**
*Excellent Parisian butcher.*
Boucherie des Provinces
20, rue d'Aligre
75012 Paris
Tel.: +33 (0)1 43 43 91 64

**Jacques Genin**
*One of Paris's most renowned pâtissiers-chocolatiers.*
La Chocolaterie
133, rue de Turenne
75003 Paris
Tel.: +33 (0)1 45 77 29 01

**Issé et Cie**
*Japanese grocery store.*
11, rue Saint-Augustin
75002 Paris
Tel.: +33 (0)1 42 96 26 74
www.isse-et-cie.fr

**Stéphane Meyer**
*Fresh organic produce.*
Benti le Bio
83, rue du Château des Rentiers
75013 Paris
Tel.: +33 (0)1 53 61 05 41

**Jean-Luc Poujauran**
*The finest bread in Paris is now available only by wholesale.*
Boulangerie Poujauran
18, rue Jean Nicot
75007 Paris
Tel.: +33 (0)1 47 05 80 88

**Bénédicte and Benoit Poisot**
*Our trusted supplier of chicken and fattened hens.*
Les Poulardes de Culoiseau
La Bertinière
61110 Moutiers-au-Perche
Tel.: +33 (0)2 33 73 87 36

**La Tête dans les Olives**
*Premium-quality Sicilian olive oil.*
2, rue Sainte-Marthe
75010 Paris
Tel.: +33 (0)9 51 31 33 34
www.latetedanslesolives.com

### DECOR

**Jean-Louis Bravo**
*A treasure trove of secondhand equipment and furniture.*
La Brocante d'Épinay
145, route de Saint-Leu
93800 Épinay-sur-Seine
Tel.: +33 (0)1 48 23 57 30
www.brocante-bravo.com

**Drucker**
*The world's oldest rattan bistro chair manufacturer.*
27, rue de l'Automne
60129 Gilocourt
Tel.: +33 (0)3 44 88 32 92
www.drucker.fr

**Pierre Sabria**
*The interior designer behind the decor of the Paul Bert and L'Écailler du Bistrot.*
78, boulevard Diderot
75012 Paris
Tel.: +33 (0)6 88 72 68 06
pierresabria.free.fr

# Recipe Index

# One Last Word

We have reached the end of the book, but I am unable to draw it to a close without thanking the starring members of its cast: the bistro owners. In order of appearance: Olivier Gaslin (Le Villaret), Raquel Carena (the Baratin), Stéphane Jego (L'Ami Jean), Cyril Bordarier (Le Verre Volé), Bernard Fontenille (L'Abordage), Gwenaëlle Cadoret (L'Écailler du Bistrot), Yves Camdeborde (Le Comptoir), Rodolphe Paquin (the Repaire de Cartouche), Christophe Acker (the Gorgeon), Benoît Gauthier (Le Grand Pan), Francis Bonfilou (the Marsangy), and Gilles Bénard (the Quedubon). At the helm of their bistros, they provide an essential link in the chain of a farming community that's in the process of rebuilding itself via its breeders, true winemakers, small-scale horticultural producers, wild herb pickers, fishermen, and oyster farmers. A big thank you to all our suppliers and all the chefs who love exceptional products and who change their menus daily, following the rhythm of the seasons.

An especially big thank you to Thierry Laurent and his crew who keep a watchful eye on the Paul Bert's tables, and to Tonny Ducrocq at L'Écailler du Bistrot. Thank you to the servers, to the dishwashers, and to all those who play their part in the success of our bistros.

Finally, one last word for all those, too numerous to mention, who are not in this book, but whose names, as they know, can be read between the lines.

Bertrand Auboyneau

Translated from the French by Carmella Abramowitz-Moreau   Design: Isabelle Ducat   Copyediting: Helen Woodhall
Typesetting: Gravemaker+Scott   Proofreading: Magda Schmit   Editorial Assistance: Carrie Benton
Color Separation: IGS, France   Printed in Italy by Grafiche Flaminia

Simultaneously published in French as Bistrot   © Flammarion, S.A., Paris, 2011

English-language edition   © Flammarion, S.A., Paris, 2012

editions.flammarion.com

12  13  14    3  2  1

ISBN: 978-2-08-020088-4

Dépôt légal: 02/2012